ETERNAL GREECE

ETERNAL GREECE

TEXT BY REX WARNER

93 PICTURES IN PHOTOGRAVURE
6 COLOUR PLATES
BY MARTIN HÜRLIMANN

A STUDIO BOOK · THE VIKING PRESS
NEW YORK

FIRST PUBLISHED 1953
REPRINTED 1955
NEW EDITION 1961

CONTENTS

PLATES

INTRODUCTION

EVERY AGE will form its own picture of Greece, but this does not mean that all the pictures will be equally accurate or informative. It is, for example, no longer possible to maintain that the statue of Laocoön represents in any true sense the spirit of Greek art of the classical period. One must look farther than a single statue or piece of architecture, however evocative of some contemporary emotion. In fact one will not understand the art without some understanding of the people, the literature, the landscape and the light. And in all of these one will observe not only a brilliance, a clarity and a most singular grace, but also a bewildering, immense and magnificent variety. Thus, while one rightly admires the qualities of balance and lucidity in the achieve-ments of the Greeks, one must be prepared always for the unexpected and the incalculable.

One must be prepared too for the contradictory. Very often, as I have watched the mountains or the sea of Greece it has occurred to me that some word such as 'real' or 'genuine' would most aptly describe the scene. For there is nothing, absolutely nothing, theatrical, sentimental or weak about the Greek landscape. But then, perhaps, the shadows of clouds will go flying over the mountain slopes, or the setting sun put a wreath of violet around the city in the plain, and in a moment there will be magic and softness in the air. So one admires a reality which is neither stark nor brutal, an enchantment in which there is no element of illusion. Add to this the knowledge that there are all kinds of visible enchantments and visible realities, and one will be the better able to understand that in classical art itself the balance is a balance of stresses and of tension, and that the achievements of this brilliant people are no more an example of abstract mathematics than is the growth of a flower from the earth or the regular and solemn motions of the sun and the stars.

Then there are the people too to consider, the creators of this art and of the greatest and most pervasive of world civilizations. Here again it is impossible to form a picture that can have the least claim to accuracy unless one is prepared for an infinite variety and innumerable contradictions. There is a picture drawn by some schoolmasters. It is of a greatly talented race of intellectuals and of athletes, devoted to the pursuit of beauty and of know-ledge, living serenely like gods, sound minds in sound bodies, avoiding the immoderate, though occasionally and most surprisingly led into deplorable excesses, usually under the influence of unscrupulous and ungentlemanly demagogues. Some indeed have gone so far as to equate the Greek 'καλὸς κἀγαθός' with the English notion of a 'gentleman'. Yet it is not only Alcibiades but Pericles also who differs most profoundly from Sir Henry Curtis. Indeed the picture is false, and, even without the resources of modern anthropology, can easily be recognized as such by anyone who has read Thucydides or even Homer, where we find the chivalry and grandeur of the greatest heroes often only precariously based, and where Achilles himself practises human sacrifice at the tomb of his loved friend. The most brilliant of all the peoples of the ancient world, the Athenians themselves, condemned to death the most original of their thinkers—in spite of the fact (and here again we encounter the contradiction) that they prided themselves above all things on the tolerance and ease of their way of life. And if the excesses committed by the ancient Greeks in war and in revolution were not on the same scale as those which we have witnessed in our time, they were often, in their more limited sphere, equally brutal and equally ruthless.

And yet the schoolmaster's picture is not a pure fabrication based on nothing. The splendid civilization did exist. Literature and art and the words of Pericles are there to prove it. We are right to be astounded at the intellectual zest and brilliance of the times, the daring, the enterprise and the innovations. It is true also that in all this stress and struggle the aim was towards a kind of harmony that would include and establish both truth and beauty without weakness or affectation. We shall understand this harmony all the better if we have some realization of the divergencies from which it is composed and of the ambitious zeal with which it was sought after.

Take, for instance, the contrast, of which the Greeks themselves were very conscious, between the Ionian and the Dorian manners and way of life.

CAPE SUNIUM or Cape Colonna, southern promontory of Attica between the open sea and the bay.
THE TEMPLE OF POSEIDON, a Doric periptery of white coarse-grained local marble. The temple is about 103 ft. long and 44 ft. broad. The columns are 20 ft. in height and have sixteen flutings each, instead of the twenty that are usual in Doric temples. There were six columns at the two ends of the temple and thirteen along the sides. The temple was built in the 5th century B.C., rather later than the Parthenon and the Theseum in Athens.

Athens and Sparta were the recognized protagonists of these races and traditions. In a debate at Sparta before the great war between the two States, the Corinthian allies of Sparta attempted to impress upon the Spartans the enormous difference of outlook which characterized the two sides. They said, according to Thucydides:

'To our minds you are quite unaware of this difference; you have never yet tried to imagine what sort of people these Athenians are against whom you will have to fight—how much, indeed how completely, different from you. An Athenian is always an innovator, quick to form a resolution and quick at carrying it out. You, on the other hand, are good at keeping things as they are; you never originate an idea, and your action tends to stop short of its aim. Then again, Athenian daring will outrun its own resources; they will take risks against their better judgment and still, in the midst of danger, remain confident. But your nature is always to do less than you could have done, to mistrust your own judgment, however sound it may be, and to assume that dangers will last for ever. Think of this too: while you are hanging back, they never hesitate; while you stay at home, they are always abroad; for they think that the farther they go the more they will get, while you think that any movement may endanger what you have already. If they win a victory, they follow it up at once, and if they suffer a defeat, they scarcely fall back at all. As for their bodies, they regard them as expendable for their city's sake, as though they were not their own; but each man cultivates his own intelligence, again with a view to doing something notable for his city. If they aim at something and do not get it, they think that they have been deprived of what belonged to them already; whereas, if their enterprise is successful, they regard that success as nothing compared to what they will do next. Suppose they fail in some undertaking; they make good the loss immediately by setting their hopes in some other direction. Of them alone it may

---

HEAD OF THE 'BLOND EPHEBE', found on the Acropolis in 1887. Parian marble with traces of colour (hair, yellow ochre; lips, eyelids and tear ducts, light red; eyebrows, black; iris, yellow-brown; pupils, black). Date about 490–480 B.C. Like the 'Critius boy', one of the most beautiful and best preserved works of the severe style. Acropolis Museum, Athens.

---

be said that they possess a thing almost as soon as they have begun to desire it, so quickly with them does action follow upon decision. And so they go on working away in hardship and danger all the days of their lives, seldom enjoying their possessions because they are always adding to them. Their view of a holiday is to do what needs doing; they prefer hardship and activity to peace and quiet. In a word, they are by nature incapable of either living a quiet life themselves or of allowing anyone else to do so.'

There is, of course, something rhetorical in the contrasting colours of this picture. Moreover it should be observed that in architecture and in literature it was the Ionian Athenians themselves who brought to its full glory the style and spirit of the Dorians. Yet in so emphasizing the ferment and the restless unceasing activity of his own people and in contrasting it with the lethargy of a conservative tradition, Thucydides not only helps to explain the history of his times but reminds us of a quality which is inherent in all creation and in all growth, a revolutionary quality which in its excess has been typified in such figures as Milton's Satan or the Prometheus of Aeschylus but which must in some sense be present if there is to be any new thing under the sun.

In the great period of ancient Greece most of the new things were of Athenian origin. Indeed, however often it is repeated, one cannot cease being astounded at the fact that in this small city some three generations of men not only laid the foundations but in many cases set the standard for the whole subsequent civilization of Europe. And there was nothing cold, nothing bleak or remote in the splendid order which they imposed on their thought and on the materials in which they worked. This order, this balance, this kind of peace and security has been achieved in disorder, disagreement, antithesis, stress and strife.

Certainly the order and the peace are real. And here we meet another antithesis: the innovators have their own conservatism; the adventurers

KOUROS, FROM CAPE SUNIUM. Dedicatory statue of a youth, about 10 ft. high. Marble (with plaster renovations on the face, arms and legs). Found at the Temple of Poseidon in 1906. Date, about 600 B.C. Now in the National Museum, Athens. An example of the early archaic style at its zenith.

respect the calm that in real life they have hardly ever known. Even in the moment of their wildest ambition the Athenian people will elect a Nicias for their general, admiring in him the qualities of sobriety and caution in which they themselves, at the time, are so conspicuously lacking. And to the same audience of Athenian citizens Euripides, the daring thinker, the critic of gods and of conventional prejudice, will, in a chorus from his *Medea*, speak of a race of people who, in the ideal imagination, are like gods themselves. And these people are the same Athenians who in fact are continually engaged in foreign war and in every kind of domestic rivalry and strife. He writes of them as 'the children of Erechtheus' and, by using the name of this legendary king, emphasizes not their modernity but their antiquity. And in the lines which follow he has nothing to say of their democracy, their imperialism, or their inventions; he speaks instead of wisdom, of love and of harmony. The lines are as follows:

> 'From of old the children of Erechtheus are
> Splendid, the sons of blessed gods. They dwell
> In Athens' holy and unconquered land
> Where famous Wisdom feeds them, and they pass gaily
> Always through that most brilliant air where once, they say,
> That golden Harmony gave birth to the nine
> Pure muses of Pieria,
>
> And beside the sweet flow of Cephisos' stream
> Where Cypris sailed, they say, to draw the water,
> And mild soft breezes breathed along her path,
> And on her hair were flung the sweet-smelling garlands
> Of flowers of roses by the Loves, the companions
> Of Wisdom, her escort, the helpers of men
> In every kind of excellence.'

STELE FROM CAPE SUNIUM, showing an ephebe placing on his head the garland of victory. The height of this fragment is 2 ft. and the work is done in marble, with traces of colour. The garland was probably of metal. Attic. Date, about 475 B.C., transition period from the archaic style to the severe style from the time of the Persian Wars.

This dignified and glorious vision of Athens and the Athenians is, in its own way, as true as is the picture given by Thucydides of restless and unceasing enterprise, of a race of busy-bodies intolerant of the idea of a quiet life. And we shall find that in the words and actions of Pericles the two pictures are somehow reconciled. Athenian democratic imperialism is justified by Athenian supremacy in thought, in art, in literature and in the skill of government. It is a dangerous argument, and it did not commend itself to the other Greeks, most of whom had as keen a sense of their own liberties as the Athenians themselves. But it is an argument which, in the case of Athens, is still very nearly convincing. Certainly it is tempting to speculate on what might have been the history of the world if, in the critical period of the war between Athens and Sparta, Athenian ambition had not been thwarted by the jealousies and inefficiencies of Athenian party strife. The mere retention of Alcibiades in the command against Syracuse might well have led to the achievement of his far-reaching plans. After conquering Sicily, Carthage, the mainland and the coasts of Hellas, Athens might have founded a Mediterranean empire too strong to have been overthrown either by Macedon or by Rome. As it was, though her military and political power was broken, Athens has remained the school not only of Hellas but of European civilization, transforming and civilizing not only the Macedonians and the Romans but every other race which has entered upon the field of history.

And here again one is faced by a paradox. It is right to remember the extraordinary rapidity with which something near perfection was reached in so many fields of art, thought and literature between the beginning of the fifth and the middle of the fourth century B.C. Yet even so, neither Athens nor Greece can be fitly represented by a few generations, however brilliant. We must remember that even at the time of Euripides the Athenians felt themselves to be not only the most modern, but also the most ancient of the peoples of Hellas. There are still today fragments of Mycenean architecture in the walls of the Acropolis. And just as the history and culture of the age of Pericles rested itself on a long and varied tradition, so the history and achievement of the Greeks extend from that point prodigiously into the future and into the present. There are other Greek cities besides Athens, and among them are Alexandria and Constantinople. Nor is it only against the Kings Darius and Xerxes that Greeks have fought magnificently for independence. Byron, unreasonably, deplored the disappearance of 'the Pyrrhic phalanx'; he would have applauded the achievements of the Albanian campaign.

Nor, to my mind, are these considerations worthless to one who looks at a statue or a piece of architecture made at a particular time and in a particular place. When we say that the achievements of the Greeks or that Greece herself is 'eternal' we mean, among many other things, that the place and spirit, even the achievements themselves, extend both forwards and backwards in time.

We also mean to suggest by the word 'eternal' a quality of intense and radiant life, something that scarcely suits with a museum, or at any rate, a museum in northern Europe. Indeed, of all the many depredations from Greece the horses from Piraeus which now adorn St Mark's in Venice seem to be the only ones which have found a fitting sanctuary. Certainly I can never see the Elgin marbles in the British Museum without wishing that a generous, or even an enlightened government would take steps to restore them to their proper place; nor can I follow the argument of those who say that it is 'better' for these marbles to be seen in the wrong light, in the wrong place, at the wrong elevation and by the wrong people simply because such people are numerous. In fact museums are not always enlightening and however necessary it may be to put statues in cages, it must still be remembered that they were meant for a free and brilliant air and to be seen against a landscape that is absolutely unique.

Sea, rocks and islands, that golden light, the perfume of aromatic shrubs— none of these are to be found inside the walls of a museum. Yet often these things are recalled to the mind's eye by those grave or smiling statues that, even in their incarceration, contain their own strength and diffuse the brilliance of their native places.

SUNIUM

IT IS said that in ancient times those who rounded Cape Sunium, coming from the north on the voyage to Piraeus, could see, under the right conditions, the sunlight glinting on the spear of the huge statue of Athena Promachus standing on the distant Acropolis. Such travellers may have been Athenian citizens returning from some military and naval expedition, from Byzantium or Thrace or the distant cities on the Black Sea. They would often have been the crews of ships carrying corn and other imports from the Hellespont; for it was on this traffic that imperial Athens depended for her life.

The first temple at Sunium was incomplete at the time when it was destroyed by the Persians. Late in the fifth century was built the white temple to Poseidon, remains of which can be seen today. In the year 413, after the great Athenian disaster in Sicily, the place was fortified, so alarmed were the Athenians for the safety of their corn-route. It was fortified again in recent years by the Germans and the Italians.

A short time ago I wrote the following description of the place:

'At distant Sunium itself the white temple of Poseidon is superbly situated to dominate the approaches to Athens from the sea. The Doric columns, of which twelve are still standing, have a lean and athletic appearance very different from the robust grace of the columns of the Parthenon. Here, on this high promontory, the temple seems to stand like a diver, stripped, and ready to dive or, since it is divine, to fly into the air.' (*Views of Attica*, p. 142.)

Writing at about the same time, Mr Osbert Lancaster gives a somewhat different impression:

'The temple, a Doric hexastyle of which barely a dozen columns are still erect, while creating a very fine effect from the sea is, as Lord Byron remarked, less impressive when seen from the land. Indeed, from the motor road it appears, when silhouetted against the sun, remarkably like a half-finished

---

CAPE SUNIUM. THE TEMPLE OF POSEIDON.

hangar; an unfortunate impression which the recent demolitions carried out by the Germans, who, with their usual enthusiasm for the treasures of antiquity, had maintained a large ammunition dump on the site, does little to diminish.' (*Classical Landscape*, p. 86.)

What is characteristic of the Greek landscape is that both these descriptions are true. The view has merely been described from very slightly different angles.

But it is from the temple itself that the view is finest. Standing among the columns, upon which innumerable travellers have cut or scratched their undistinguished names (though here we except Lord Byron, who must have spent many hours over the carving of his very large and durable autograph) one can look away to the south over the small island of St George, which lies close to the promontory, and see in the distance the coast of the Argolid and the indomitable island of Hydra, or, farther eastward, the Cyclades—Keos, Tenos, Andros and Melos. It is the sea over which Athens was supreme, and inland, not far from Sunium, is the mining district of Laurion, the revenues from which were, on the advice of Themistocles, used to lay the foundation of Athenian naval power.

With such astonishing energy was this power used that, within thirty years of the destruction of Athens by the Persians, this city had become the greatest power in the Mediterranean and was beginning to adorn herself like a queen.

CAPE SUNIUM. View from the south front of the Temple of Poseidon across the sea.

THE BUILDING OF ATHENS

T HE VAST building programme undertaken by Pericles and his advisers was largely financed by the contributions of the allies of Athens to a general fund which, at any rate originally, was intended to be used to equip military and naval forces to preserve the Greeks from subjugation to Persia. The political opponents of Pericles in Athens may or may not have realized that, as the Parthenon and the Propylaea were being built, their city was being enriched with two buildings of incomparable beauty, two wonders of the world. Whether or not they were aware of this fact, their view was, according to Plutarch, that:

'Greece cannot but resent it as an insufferable affront, and consider herself to be tyrannized over openly, when she sees the treasure which was contributed by her upon a necessity for the war, wantonly lavished out by us upon our city, to gild her all over, and to adorn and set her forth, as it were some vain woman, hung round with precious stones and figures and temples, which cost a world of money.' (*Life of Pericles*. Tr. Dryden.)

Pericles' reply to this was that, so long as the allies were defended, they were getting what they paid for. And Athens was, to him, an end in itself. So the work went on, and is described as follows by Plutarch:

'The materials were stone, brass, ivory, gold, ebony, cypress-wood; and the arts or trades that wrought and fashioned them were smiths and carpenters, moulders, founders, braziers, stone-cutters, dyers, goldsmiths, ivory-workers, painters, embroiderers, turners; those again that conveyed them to the town for use, merchants and mariners and ship-masters by sea, and by land, cart-wrights, cattle-breeders, waggoners, rope-makers, flax-workers, shoemakers and leather-dressers, road-makers, miners. And every trade in the same nature, as a captain in an army has his particular company of soldiers under him, had its own hired company of journeymen and labourers belonging to it banded together as in array, to be as it were the instrument and body for the perfor-mance of the service. Thus, to say all in a word, the occasion and services of these public works distributed plenty through every age and condition.

'As then grew the works up, no less stately in size than exquisite in form, the workmen striving to outvie the material and the design with the beauty of their workmanship, yet the most wonderful thing of all was the rapidity of their execution.

'Undertakings, any one of which singly might have required, they thought, for their completion, several successions and ages of men, were every one of them accomplished in the height and prime of one man's political service. Although they say, too, that Zeuxis once, having heard Agatharchus the painter boast of despatching his work with speed and ease, replied, "I take a long time." For ease and speed in doing a thing do not give the work lasting solidity or exactness of beauty; the expenditure of time allowed to a man's pains beforehand for the production of a thing is repaid by way of interest with a vital force for the preservation when once produced. For which reason Pericles' works are especially admired, as having been made quickly, to last long. For every particular piece of his work was immediately, even at that time, for its beauty and elegance, antique; and yet in its vigour and freshness looks to this day as if it were just executed. There is a sort of bloom of newness upon those works of his, preserving them from the touch of time, as if they had some perennial spirit and undying vitality mingled in the composition of them.

'Phidias had the oversight of all the works, and was surveyor-general, though upon the various portions other great masters and workmen were employed. Callicrates and Ictinus built the Parthenon. . . . The Propylaea, or entrances to the Acropolis, were finished in five years' time, Mnesicles being the principal architect. A strange accident happened in the course of building, which showed that the goddess was not averse to the work, but was aiding and co-operating to bring it to perfection. One of the artificers, the quickest and the handiest workman among them all, with a slip of his foot fell down from a great height, and lay in a miserable condition, the physicians having no hope of his recovery. When Pericles was in distress about this, Minerva appeared to him at night in a dream, and ordered a course of treat-ment, which he applied, and in a short time and with great ease cured the man. And upon this occasion it was that he set up a brass statue of Minerva, surnamed Health, in the citadel near the altar, which they say was there before.

'But it was Phidias who wrought the goddess's image in gold, and he has his name inscribed on the pedestal as the workman of it; and indeed the whole work in a manner was under his charge, and he had, as we have said already, the oversight over all the artists and workmen, through Pericles' friendship for him; and this, indeed, made him much envied, and his patron shamefully slandered with stories, as if Phidias were in the habit of receiving, for Pericles' use, freeborn women that came to see the works. The comic writers of the town, when they had got hold of this story, made much of it, and bespattered him with all the ribaldry they could invent, charging him falsely with the wife of Menippus, one who was his friend and served as lieutenant under him in the wars; and with the birds kept by Pyrilampes, an acquaintance of Pericles, who, they pretended, used to give presents of peacocks to Pericles' female friends.' (*Life of Pericles*. Tr. Dryden.)

THE ACROPOLIS, ATHENS, with the Parthenon (centre), seen from the south-west. *Below:* THE ACROPOLIS. Approach from the west, showing the Propylaea, the Temple of Nike, and the Parthenon in the background, right.
(*Pages 26–7*) THE ACROPOLIS, ATHENS. View from the west, showing the Propylaea, the Temple of Nike and the Parthenon. To the left of the Acropolis is Mount Lycabettus.

THE IDEAL OF ATHENS

SCANDALOUS stories about peacocks, references to the ridiculous shape of Pericles' head—these things delighted the comic poets and their audiences. Yet to Pericles himself there happened what, if we can judge the man from what we know of him, he would have wished for himself more than any other gift. He is immortal in the pages of Thucydides and in these pages his immortality rests on his own words of love to Athens, and his own record in the service of that love.

When, at the end of the first year of that disastrous war between Athens and Sparta, Pericles, as a man 'chosen by the city for his intellectual gifts and for his general reputation', came forward and stood upon a high platform to speak the conventional speech in memory of those who had fallen in their country's service, he spoke for the moment and for all time. No doubt, though the work was still so new, some of those young men, whose figures we can see today riding their horses in the frieze of the Parthenon, had lost their lives in the plain of Parnes or at Potidaea or round the Peloponnesian coast. When near his end, Pericles is said to have regarded as his greatest virtue the fact that 'no Athenian, through my means, ever wore mourning'. Yet in the struggle to preserve what Athens was and to make Athens greater still he was ready enough to venture both his own and other people's lives. No statesman in history has made such claims for his country (and yet the claims are true); none has spoken with so dispassionate an accuracy words charged with such burning zeal. Among other things he said in this famous speech:

'Our system of government does not copy the institutions of our neighbours. It is more the case of our being a model to others, than of our imitating anyone else. Our constitution is called a democracy because power is in the

---

MOSCOPHORUS (Calf-carrier) FROM THE ACROPOLIS. Dedicatory statue representing a herdsman carrying a calf. Found in 1864. Hymettus marble with traces of colour, and eyes formerly inset. Archaic Attic work dating from about 570–560 B.C. Height, together with limestone plinth (found in 1887), 5 ft. 5 in. Acropolis Museum, Athens.

---

hands not of a minority but of the whole people. When it is a question of settling private disputes, everyone is equal before the law; when it is a question of putting one person before another in positions of public responsibility, what counts is not membership of a particular class, but the actual ability which the man possesses. No one, so long as he has it in him to be of service to the state, is kept in political obscurity because of poverty. And, just as our political life is free and open, so is our day-to-day life in our relations with each other. We do not get into a state with our next-door neighbour if he enjoys himself in his own way, nor do we give him the kind of black looks which, though they do no real harm, still do hurt people's feelings. We are free and tolerant in our private lives; but in public affairs we keep to the law. This is because it commands our deep respect. . . .

'And here is another point. When our work is over, we are in a position to enjoy all kinds of recreation for our spirits. There are various kinds of contests and sacrifices regularly throughout the year; in our own homes we find a beauty and a good taste which delight us every day and which drive away our cares. Then the greatness of our city brings it about that all the good things from all over the world flow in to us, so that to us it seems just as natural to enjoy foreign goods as our own local products.

'Then there is a great difference between us and our opponents, in our attitude towards military security. Here are some examples: Our city is open to the world, and we have no periodical deportations in order to prevent people observing or finding out secrets which might be of military advantage to the enemy. This is because we rely, not on secret weapons, but on our own real courage and loyalty. There is a difference, too, in our educational systems. The Spartans, from their earliest boyhood, are submitted to the most laborious training in courage; we pass our lives without all these restrictions, and yet are just as ready to face the same dangers as they are. . . . There are certain advantages, I think, in our way of meeting danger voluntarily, with an easy mind, instead of with a laborious training, with natural rather than with

---

KORE, VOTIVE OFFERING of Eutydicus, found 1882-6 on the Acropolis near the Erechtheum. Parian marble, with traces of colour (hair, eyes and lips red, polos blue). Height of torso 22⅞ in. Date, about 490-480 B.C., transition from attic late-archaic to severe style. Acropolis Museum, Athens.

state-induced courage. We do not have to spend our time practising to meet sufferings which are still in the future; and when they are actually upon us we show ourselves just as brave as these others who are always in strict training. This is one point in which, I think, our city deserves to be admired. There are also others:

'Our love of what is beautiful does not lead to extravagance; our love of the things of the mind does not make us soft. We regard wealth as something to be properly used, rather than as something to boast about. As for poverty, no one need be ashamed to admit it: the real shame is in not taking practical measures to escape from it. Here each individual is interested not only in his own affairs but in the affairs of the state as well: even those who are mostly occupied with their own business are extremely well informed on general politics—this is a peculiarity of ours: we do not say that a man who takes no interest in politics is a man who minds his own business; we say that he has no business here at all. We Athenians, in our own persons, take our decisions on policy or submit them to proper discussions: for we do not think that there is an incompatibility between words and deeds; the worst thing is to rush into action before the consequences have been properly debated. . . .

'Taking everything together then, I declare that our city is an education to Greece, and I declare that in my opinion each single one of our citizens, in all the manifold aspects of life is able to show himself the rightful lord and owner of his own person, and do this, moreover, with exceptional grace and exceptional versatility. And to show that this is no empty boasting for the present occasion, but real tangible fact, you have only to consider the power which our city possesses and which has been won by those very qualities which I have mentioned. Athens, alone of the states we know, comes to her testing time in a greatness that surpasses what was imagined of her. In her case, and in her case alone, no invading enemy is ashamed at being defeated, and no subject can complain of being governed by people unfit for their responsibilities. Mighty indeed are the marks and monuments of our empire which we have

---

HORSE FROM THE ACROPOLIS. Head of a horse (standing), probably the votive offering of a rider. Found near the Erechtheum in 1887. Parian marble with traces of colour (mane and mouth, red; eyes, grey-blue). Height of horse 3¾ ft. Date, about 500 B.C. Acropolis Museum, Athens.

---

left. Future ages will wonder at us, as the present age wonders at us now. We do not need the praises of a Homer, or of anyone else whose words may delight us for the moment, but whose estimation of facts will fall short of what is really true. For our adventurous spirit has forced an entry into every sea and into every land; and everywhere we have left behind us everlasting memorials of good done to our friends or suffering inflicted on our enemies.

'This, then, is the kind of city for which these men, who could not bear the thought of losing her, nobly fought and nobly died. It is only natural that every one of us who survive them should be willing to undergo hardships in her service. And it was for this reason that I have spoken at such length about our city, because I wanted to make it clear that for us there is more at stake than there is for others who lack our advantages; also I wanted my words of praise for the dead to be set in the bright light of evidence. And now the most important of these words has been spoken. I have sung the praises of our city; but it was the courage and gallantry of these men, and of people like them, which made her splendid. Nor would you find it true in the case of many of the Greeks, as it is true of them, that no words can do more than justice to their deeds. . . .

'No one of these men weakened because he wanted to go on enjoying his wealth: no one put off the awful day in the hope that he might live to escape his poverty and grow rich. More to be desired than such things, they chose to check the enemy's pride. This, to them, was a risk most glorious, and they accepted it, willing to strike down the enemy and relinquish everything else. As for success or failure, they left that in the doubtful hands of Hope, and when the reality of battle was before their faces, they put their trust in their own selves. In the fighting, they thought it more honourable to stand their ground and suffer death than to give in and save their lives. So they fled from the reproaches of men, abiding with life and limb the brunt of battle; and, in a small moment of time, the climax of their lives, a culmination of glory, not of fear, were swept away from us.

THE PARTHENON, north frieze; youths carrying water vessels. Acropolis Museum, Athens.
(Pages 36–7) THE PARTHENON. View from the interior through the columns at the north-east corner, across the city to Mount Lycabettus.

'So and such they were, these men—worthy of their city. We who remain behind may hope to be spared their fate, but must resolve to keep the same daring spirit against the foe. It is not simply a question of estimating the advantages in theory. I could tell you a long story (and you know it as well as I do) about what is to be gained by beating the enemy back. What I would prefer is that you should fix your eyes every day on the greatness of Athens as she really is, and should fall in love with her. When you realize her greatness, then reflect that what made her great was men with a spirit of adventure, men who knew their duty, men who were ashamed to fall below a certain standard. If they ever failed in an enterprise, they made up their minds that at any rate the city should not find their courage lacking to her, and they gave to her the best contribution that they could. They gave her their lives, to her and to all of us, and for their own selves they won praises that never grow old, the most splendid of sepulchres—not the sepulchre in which their bodies are laid, but where their glory remains eternal in men's minds, always there on the right occasion to stir others to speech or to action. For famous men have the whole earth as their memorial: it is not only the inscriptions on their graves in their own country that mark them out; no, in foreign lands also, not in any visible form but in people's hearts, their memory abides and grows. . . .

'It is impossible for a man to put forward fair and honest views about our affairs if he has not, like everyone else, children whose lives may be at stake. As for those of you who are now too old to have children, I would ask you to count as gain the greater part of your life, in which you have been happy, and remember that what remains is not long, and let your hearts be lifted up at the thought of the fair fame of the dead. One's sense of honour is the only thing that does not grow old, and the last pleasure, when one is worn out with age, is not, as the poet said, making money, but having the respect of one's fellow men.

'As for those of you here who are sons or brothers of the dead, I can see a hard struggle in front of you. Everyone always speaks well of the dead, and, even if you rise to the greatest heights of heroism, it will be a hard thing for

---

THE PARTHENON FRIEZE. *Above:* Poseidon, Apollo and Artemis, from the representation of the Olympian gods on the east frieze. Acropolis Museum, Athens. *Below:* Riders from the cavalcade on the west frieze. (Photographed *in situ*; photo by Boissonnas.)

---

you to get the reputation of having come near, let alone equalled, their standard. When one is alive, one is always liable to the jealousy of one's competitors, but when one is out of the way, the honour one receives is sincere and unchallenged.

'Perhaps I should say a word or two on the duties of women to those among you who are now widowed. I can say all I have to say in a short word of advice. Your great glory is not to be inferior to what God has made you, and the greatest glory of a woman is to be least talked about by men, whether they are praising you or criticizing you. I have now, as the law demanded, said what I had to say. For the time being our offerings to the dead have been made, and for the future their children will be supported at the public expense by the city, until they come of age. This is the crown and prize which she offers, both to the dead and to their children, for the ordeals which they have faced. Where the rewards of valour are the greatest, there you will find also the best and bravest spirits among the people. And now, when you have mourned for your dear ones, you must depart.'

EQUESTRIAN STATUE FROM THE ACROPOLIS, representing a rider with a garland of oak leaves. Parian marble. Date, about 550 B.C. The so-called 'Rampin Head' in the Louvre (found in 1877) and the torso found near the Erechtheum in 1886 were pieced together by Payne. Height of head 11⅜ in., of torso 2 ft. 8 in. Louvre (torso in replica).

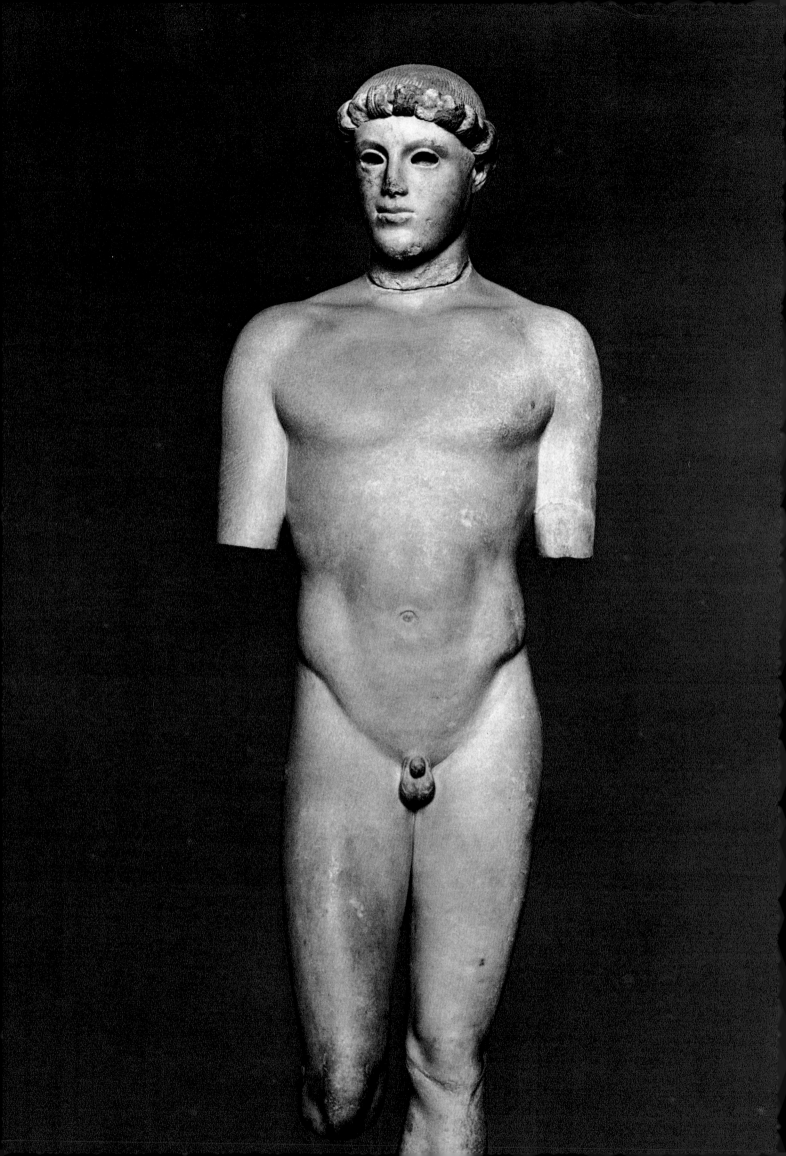

FESTIVALS

O F THE 'contests and sacrifices' which throughout the year took place in ancient Athens for the recreation and good of her citizens, two in particular—the city Dionysia and the Panathenaic procession—have left visible remains in art and architecture.

It is said that the tyrant Pisistratus brought the god Dionysus to Athens in the sixth century from Eleutherae, the frontier post between Attica and Boeotia, on the slopes of Mount Cithaeron. This mountain and the city of Thebes in the plain beyond are associated with the legend of Pentheus, the king who, on the practical grounds of efficiency and common sense, refused to recognize the existence and the validity of the god Dionysus and of his ecstatic rites. As a result of this impious attitude he was torn to pieces by his mother and by his aunts. In Athens, however, the character of the god was different. He was connected with fertility and he had his place in the Mysteries of Demeter and Persephone at Eleusis; but in particular he was associated with the theatre, with the invention of the arts of tragedy and comedy.

His temple was on the southern slopes of the Acropolis. Near the temple wooden benches were erected round an orchestra where the first performances of drama, rude enough, in all probability, were given. Here again a short time was sufficient to achieve a kind of perfection. Yet it was still in this old wooden theatre that the plays of Aeschylus, Sophocles and Euripides were first produced. The grey stone theatre which can be seen today was not constructed until the fourth century. It was capable of holding more than fifteen thousand spectators, yet it still has an air of intimacy, something which would befit a religious and social occasion, and in this respect differs greatly from the vast theatre of Epidaurus.

There were several festivals throughout the year held in honour of Dionysus. In December came the rustic Dionysia, held in all the rural districts of

---

'CRITIUS BOY', statue of an ephebe, pieced together by H. Schrader from a torso found on the Acropolis in 1865 and a head found there in 1888. Probably the statue of a victor in an athletic contest. Parian marble. Height 2 ft. 10 in. Date, about 480 B.C., probably an early work from the workshop of Critius and Nesiotes. Acropolis Museum, Athens.

Attica. There were dramatic performances, a procession in which phalli were carried, obscene songs and much shouting and merry-making. It is a festival which may well have influenced the Roman Saturnalia, held in the same month, from which much of the tradition of our own Christmas festivities is derived. Then, in January, came the feast of the Lenaea or feast of the wine-vats, again celebrated with a procession and dramatic performances. In February, when the casks were opened and the new wine was tasted, came the three-day festival of the Anthesteria, a festival of flowers. The most important day was called 'The Jugs'. The wine was blessed by Dionysus, and everyone, including the small children, carried away his own jug of wine to drink. On the same day a statue of Dionysus was brought in on a ship on wheels and was symbolically married to the wife of the King-Archon. After the merry-making, however, the character of the festival changed, and in the evening sacrifices were made to the dead. But the greatest of these festivals was the city Dionysia, held about March. At this festival the great performances of tragedy and comedy were given for three days on end in the theatre by the Acropolis, and from all over Greece people flocked to attend. Here also the ceremonies began with a gorgeous procession in which the statue of Dionysus was carried to his temple near the theatre, and in the evening, after the sacrifices, the god was carried out again by the young men and brought by torchlight into the theatre itself to witness the performances given in his honour.

There were other festivals too in honour of Demeter and Apollo which were celebrated in Athens. But the grandest of all was the Panathenaea which was held every year at about the end of July. It was the feast in honour of Athena herself and every fourth year it was celebrated with peculiar splendour. There were horse races and contests in music and in poetry. On the last day took place the great procession to the Acropolis and to Athena's temple, the

---

NIKE, FASTENING HER SANDAL. Marble relief, $5\frac{1}{4}$ ft. high. From the sequence of representations of that figure on the frieze of the balustrade of the Temple of Nike. About 410 B.C. Recovered in 1835, and now in the Acropolis Museum.
(Pages 46-7) THE PROPYLAEA. 46: View through the middle section, with the Erechtheum beyond. 47: View through the middle section, with the Parthenon beyond. On the left is the single rebuilt specimen of six Ionic columns, $33\frac{7}{8}$ ft. high, with twenty-four flutings. The Doric columns are 29 ft. high, and bear twenty flutings.

Parthenon, where the goddess was presented with the 'peplos', a gorgeous robe woven for her by the ladies of Athens. This procession can still be seen depicted in the Parthenon frieze. There are the maidens carrying baskets, the young men leading the animals for sacrifice, the horsemen, the whole grace and strength of a city devoted to its own ideal in the service of its own goddess. For, even if there were no other evidence, the sculptures of the Parthenon alone would convince us that the Athenians, in spite of their rationalism, believed not only in themselves but in divine powers.

Of some of these sculptures Sir Maurice Bowra writes as follows:

'The Parthenon was a temple of a goddess in whose reality men believed, and the sculptures which adorned it show what the Athenians thought about themselves. They depict partly struggles against primitive creatures like centaurs, thus illustrating the rise of Athens from uncouth barbarism, partly events of cosmic grandeur which underlie the course of Athenian history. The east pediment shows the birth of Athena on Olympus. A celestial world of dreaming calm is broken by the sudden appearance of a fully grown goddess in its midst, and wakes with awe and amazement at it. The west pediment shows the struggle of Athena and Poseidon for the possession of Attica: two great divinities in conflict, and a fearful sense of power and effort. Each pediment represents a different aspect of the national myth. If the east shows what the emergence of such a power as Athena means even on Olympus, the west shows what a goddess this must be that even the lord of the sea quails before her. This is not allegory but mythology in the truest sense. The gods in their own sphere display in a pure form what happens to the men who live under their sway. Both scenes are concerned with power, either emerging or in full action, and both present to the eye the unexampled force which the Athenians felt at work in themselves and believed to be divine.' ('Athens: the Periclean Age', from *Golden Ages of the Great Cities*.)

THE PROPYLAEA, the western entrance hall to the Acropolis of Athens. Begun by Mnesicles, on the older foundation walls, after completion of the Parthenon in 437 B.C. Pentelic marble. *Above:* East aspect seen from the Parthenon. *Below:* The western approach seen from the Temple of Nike.

FROM about the year 431 B.C. processions, worshippers and visitors to the temples of the Acropolis have passed through the Propylaea, the great porch and entrance at the west of the hill. Mnesicles was the architect and the work was begun after the completion of the Parthenon and finished in five years. The cost is said to have been 2,012 talents, or about half a million pounds.

This great gateway, with its two porticoes (one of which, in the time of Pausanias, was famous as a picture gallery) stands at the top of a steep ascent. As one climbs the hill, so every second the perspective alters and again one is struck by the contrast or rather by the union of stability and variety, of mass and of lightness which is so characteristic of the Greek scene.

Of this building Mr Osbert Lancaster writes:

'Here, quite apart from the exceptionally difficult nature of the site, the architects were faced with a far from simple task; they were to provide a fitting entrance for an enclosure which was to be at one and the same time a shrine and a fortress. Maybe the use of both the Doric and Ionic orders represents a conscious attempt to symbolize the dual nature of their task. At all events their triumph was complete; the Propylaea remains the most impressive entrance with which any man-made structure has ever been provided. Compared to this the great Gothic porches with their concentric rings of saints and their sculptured tympana appear confused, the rusticated heraldry-laden gateways of the High Renaissance bombastic. But not only is the Propylaea perfect in itself, but in addition it provides the ideal frame through which to catch one's first sight of the Parthenon.' (*Classical Landscape*, p. 44.)

TEMPLE OF NIKE on the Acropolis, Athens, dedicated to Athena Nike, or Wingless Victory. Built of Pentelic marble soon after the Propylaea, it is 27 ft. long and 18 ft. broad. The eight Ionic columns of the two small porticoes are 13 ft. high. Reconstructed from the debris of the Turkish bastions in 1835-6 by Ludwig Ross with the help of Schaubert and Hansen.

THE PARTHENON

IT IS perfectly true to say that the Parthenon is 'peripteral octastyle (columns 8 by 17), measuring 218 by 100 feet on top step of stylobate', but there are not many occasions when one thinks of it in this way. As from the Propylaea one continues to climb, though now only over a slope of grey and rough stone, and as one comes nearer and nearer to this great temple, awe rather than mathematical calculation will dominate the mind. Here whatever one may have learned from the study of photographs or whatever one may have anticipated in imagination is enormously excelled by the reality. The very proportions of the building, whether expressed in mathematical symbols or indicated by the camera, can scarcely be understood unless they have been seen with the naked eye against the stupendous background of their surroundings. For it is impossible only to see the Parthenon. Even when one looks at it closely one is conscious also of the wide ring of mountains that surround the Attic plain, of the sea in the distance, of a sky that seems higher and more extensive than the skies of northern Europe, of clouds, sunlight and limpid air. Out of all these elements seems to have grown or been distilled the beauty of the building. In the perfect place the perfect work of art has been set. In this great sanctuary of imperial Athens there is nothing grandiose, no luxury, no affectation; here is diffusion of wealth without display, control with no pettiness and no rigour; a thing which was done once and could never be done again.

DEDICATORY RELIEF TO ATHENA, the so-called 'Mourning Athena', from the Acropolis. Height 21¼ in. Parian marble with faint traces of colour. Probably the work of the great sculptor Myron. Date, about 460 B.C. Acropolis Museum, Athens. Athena, leaning on her spear, stands thoughtfully in front of a boundary-stone.

THE OTHER building on the Acropolis that still stands is the Erechtheum, the temple built in the Ionian style during the latter part of the
fifth century to replace the earlier temple which had been destroyed by the
Persians and which was dedicated to the patron deities of Athens, Athena
and Poseidon and the legendary half-divine King Erechtheus. The style of
this temple is in complete contrast to that of the Parthenon and different
opinions have been expressed of its merits.

Mr Osbert Lancaster, for instance, states that:

'to maintain an attitude of uncritical admiration before [the Erechtheum]
is to sidestep one of the most puzzling questions that arises in the whole
history of Greek architecture. How could the Greeks with their clear, logical
outlook and their unshakably humanistic standards of taste ever have tolerated,
let alone evolved, the caryatid? To them more than to any other people it
would, one would have thought, have been obvious that to employ a natura-
listic three-dimensional rendering of the human form as an architectural unit
was to invite disaster. When the Baroque architect of the seventeenth century,
whose aims were anyhow completely different, flanked a doorway with a pair
of groaning Atlases he had an expressionist justification; the over-life-size
figures with exaggeratedly bulging muscles do at least emphasize, as they were

---

THE PARTHENON, the Temple of Athena on the summit of the Acropolis, Athens,
erected on the site of a pre-Periclean building, in Pentelic marble. Architects: Ictinus and
Callicrates. The most famous of all the Doric temples. Begun in 447 B.C.; Phidias' gold-
and-ivory statue of Athena Parthenos, completed about 438/7. Its columns rise from a
three-tiered base; eight at the ends, seventeen along the sides. Their height is about 34 ft. 5$\frac{3}{8}$ in.;
diameter 6 ft. 6$\frac{3}{4}$ in.
THE FRIEZE, depicting the Panathenaic procession, was 525 ft. long and 3 ft. 3 in.
high. It was executed by various sculptors under the direction of Phidias. Two maidens and
a master of the ceremonies in the Procession of Maidens; from the east frieze, Louvre, Paris.
(Pages 56-7) THE PARTHENON FROM THE NORTH-WEST. The re-erection of
the entire range of columns was not effected until the period between the two world wars.
This was the final phase of the work of reconstruction on the Acropolis, started by Balanos
in 1902.

intended to do, the weight and mass of the architrave or balcony, which they supposedly support. But here these elegant flower maidens simper as unconcernedly as if they had never been called upon to balance two and a half tons of Pentelic marble on their pretty little heads.' (*Classical Landscape*, p. 46.)

Here, though with great respect, I would venture to differ from Mr Lancaster. After reading his book from which the above quotation has been taken I did, in fact, write as follows:

'To me the Erechtheum seems not only beautiful in itself but also aptly to illustrate that element of variety, even of contradiction, that one finds constantly in Greece. The thin Ionic columns, the careful and graceful decoration of doors and cornices—all this may be described as finicky or feminine. The different planes on which the building is constructed, the porch of the maidens which so stirs the fury of Mr Lancaster, everything seems to be made to express variety in detail, a gracious and not an overwhelming surprise. With all the profusion of decoration there is a kind of modesty about this Ionic temple to which Dorians were not allowed access. It is a place of peace and calm, a fitting sanctuary for the commemoration of the old quarrel and the lasting agreement between Athena and Poseidon. Though it invites rather than challenges or fills the eye, the invitation is, to me, both acceptable and delightful. The style recalls neither the glories of empire, the toils of war, the massive or exact triumphs of the intellect; instead the building seems to hint at the different life of island principalities, the courts of Samos or of Egypt, even Antioch and Alexandria, since this Ionic spirit, luxurious and, like the early statues of women with their delicate robes and hair, somewhat inscrutable in expression, reaches both forwards and backwards in time. It has its own purity, a purity expressed rather than impaired by what, from a strictly Dorian point of view, might appear to be vagaries or affectations. Here, on

---

THE PARTHENON. *Above:* The west front. *Below:* Auxo and Hegemone, the Athenian Charities (or Graces) worshipped at Athens, from the east pediment; larger than life-size, representing the birth of Athena. The figures on the pediment were, after the metopes and the frieze, the last sculptures carved on the Parthenon, completed 432 B.C.

---

the Acropolis, it is properly displayed in a building whose complications somehow achieve an effect of a miraculous intimacy, so that it seems, not ridiculous, but natural, however surprising, for maidens to be carrying so great a weight of marble on their heads.' (*Views of Attica*, p. 50.)

The so-called THESEUM, Athens. West façade, seen from the south-west. A remarkably well-preserved Doric temple. Probably dedicated originally to Hephaestus and Athena. Built about the same time and to a similar plan as the Parthenon, though very much smaller, it is also of Pentelic marble. The only reliable evidence is an inscription of 421 concerning the erection of the two temples.

WHETHER or not the caryatid may be described as a proper element of architecture, no one, I think, could maintain that a caryatid, removed from the porch where her sisters stand, complete with a portion of masonry which, in isolation from the rest, cannot but be wholly meaningless, and set down in the dim light of a British museum, must necessarily be offensive to the eye and disgusting to the moral sense.

It is usual to defend Lord Elgin and other collectors of the time by saying that if they had not made off with the marbles somebody else would have done so, or else the marbles would have been destroyed by the Turks. In the first of these suppositions there is certainly some truth. Yet it is an odd proposition to make—that, when there are a number of people ready to take what does not belong to them, the one who actually does so first is guiltless. There were many protests at the time against what my French guide-book of Athens describes as the 'rapines brutales de Lord Elgine'. Few were more pointed and outspoken than those of Lord Byron. In his early poem *English Bards and Scotch Reviewers* written before the famous marbles from the Acropolis had been acquired, Byron makes no secret of his dislike for collectors:

> 'Let Aberdeen and Elgin still pursue
> The shade of fame through regions of virtù;
> Waste useless thousands on their Phidian freaks,
> Misshapen monuments and maim'd antiques;
> And make their grand saloons a general mart
> For all the mutilated blocks of art.'

Above: Athens. The Ancient market-place or AGORA, seen from the northern slopes of the Acropolis, with the Theseum in the distance. *Below:* Athens. THE THEATRE OF DIONYSUS, with its rows of seats climbing the southern slopes of the Acropolis, was built in its new form on the site of an older wooden structure about 336 B.C.; but later still, under Hadrian, it was considerably altered. It held 14,000–17,000 spectators. View from the west; from right to left: the stage, in front of that the orchestra, in the middle of which stood the altar of Dionysus; then the rows of seats, the front rows, reserved for dignitaries of state, being made of marble.

Later, in 1811, he returns with much greater passion to the subject. In 'The Curse of Minerva' the poet is confronted with a vision of the great goddess of Athens herself. Thus she addresses him:

' "Mortal!"—'twas thus she spoke—"that blush of shame
Proclaims thee Briton, once a noble name;
First of the mighty, foremost of the free,
Now honoured *less* by all and *least* by me:
Chief of thy foes shall Pallas still be found.
Seek'st thou the cause of loathing?—look around.
Lo! here, despite of war and wasting fire,
I saw successive tyrannies expire.
'Scaped from the ravage of the Turk and Goth,
Thy country sends a spoiler worse than both.
Survey this vacant, violated fane;
Recount the relics torn that yet remain:
These Cecrops placed, *this* Pericles adorn'd,
That Adrian rear'd when drooping Science mourn'd.
What more I owe let gratitude attest—
Know, Alaric and Elgin did the rest.
That all may learn from whence the plunderer came,
The insulted wall sustains his hated name:
For Elgin's fame thus grateful Pallas pleads.
Below his name—above, behold his deeds!
Be ever hail'd with equal honour here
The Gothic monarch and the Pictish peer:

THE ERECHTHEUM, NORTH PORTICO. This stands on a rocky terrace, about 10 ft. lower than the rest of the building; it has six Ionic columns and rich ornamentation, especially on the doorway which leads to the sanctuary.
(Page 66) THE ERECHTHEUM, EAST PORTICO. A simple prostyle, having six Ionic columns, each 20 ft. high with twenty-four flutings. The corner column on the right was removed by Lord Elgin.
(Page 67) CARYATID FROM THE ERECHTHEUM, removed by Lord Elgin. Of Pentelic marble, $7\frac{3}{4}$ ft. high. Now in the British Museum.

Arms gave the first his right, the last had none,
But basely stole what less barbarians won." ' '

So, for some few more lines, the goddess goes on with her invective, not
even sparing the private life of Lord Elgin. Then Byron, rather conveniently
forgetting his own Scottish ancestry, replies:

'Daughter of Jove! in Britain's injured name
A true-born Briton may the deed disclaim.
Frown not on England: England owns him not:
Athena, no! thy plunderer was a Scot.'

It is doubtful whether Athena is much mollified by this defence. After
cursing the plunderer of her treasures and before involving the whole of British
foreign policy in predictions of calamity, she conjures up a vision of the scene
in London where crowds will visit and admire 'his Lordship's "stone-shop".'

'Round the throng'd gate shall sauntering coxcombs creep,
To lounge and lucubrate, to prate and peep;
While many a languid maid, with longing sigh,
On giant statues casts the curious eye;
The room with transient glance appears to skim,
Yet marks the mighty back and length of limb;
Mourns o'er the difference of *now* and *then*;
Exclaims, "These Greeks indeed were proper men!"
Draws slight comparisons of *these* with *those*,
And envies Laïs all her Attic beaux.
When shall a modern maid have swains like these!
Alas! Sir Harry is no Hercules!

THE ERECHTHEUM, PORCH OF THE MAIDENS. Facing south, it has six
figures larger than life-size supporting the balcony, the so-called 'Caryatids'. The second
figure from the left was removed by Lord Elgin and has since been replaced by a replica
(see page 67).

And last of all, amidst the gaping crew,
Some calm spectator, as he takes his view,
In silent indignation mix'd with grief,
Admires the plunder, but abhors the thief.'

The same subject is dealt with by Byron in the second Canto of *Childe Harold's Pilgrimage*, and, in the course of a note to this passage, he expresses himself, perhaps more decorously than in the passages which I have quoted, in prose. 'On this occasion,' he writes, 'I speak impartially: I am not a collector or an admirer of collections, consequently no rival; but I have some early prepossession in favour of Greece, and do not think the honour of England advanced by plunder, whether of India or Attica.'

THE PARTHENON FRIEZE. Head of a rider. Detail from section on page 72 (top), seen obliquely from the left; west frieze. British Museum, London.

THE SIN OF THE HERO HIPPOLYTUS

BOTH THE Erechtheum and the Parthenon are holy places, and the buildings on the Acropolis at Athens represented something very much more than Athenian imperialism. Contrast them with the buildings of imperial Rome, and a startling difference will be discovered. So too with the sculpture. Statues of Roman emperors or athletes cannot fail to remind us of modern business men or bruisers; but in every head, every grave relief or vase from ancient Greece there is a grace, a vitality, often a kind of mystery which can scarcely be associated with anything ordinary or vulgar in our own times. There is a feeling, not quite of spirituality, but of something very different from materialism. In spite of their rationalism these people believed in the gods and were conscious of their presence. Even their cult of athletics was a sacred cult.

There are some widely held views with regard to Greek religion which are demonstrably untrue. It has been held, for instance, that so clear-minded a people could not 'really' have believed in a multiplicity of deities. Plato and Aristotle have been approved of for their excursions in the direction of mono-theism. The mysteries have been admitted as partially respectable in so far as they expressed a doctrine of a future life. And it has been assumed that the priesthood of Delphi must have been always superstitious or corrupt, while the gods of Olympus were on the whole mere abstractions found useful in their work by sculptors and by poets.

Such views as these are contradicted by the evidence of literature, history and art. We may not like it, but we must admit the fact that on religious matters the Greeks thought and felt differently from ourselves.

There were different religions for different people at different ages and at different times. Yet there was humility and not much time-serving. Perhaps there was less arrogance than is to be found in the records of Christian churches, because there was less assurance that the ways of God could be easily or mathematically demonstrated to man as just. Certainly no one would have

---

THE PARTHENON FRIEZE. *Above:* Two riders, from the west frieze. British Museum, London. *Below:* Youths with cattle for sacrifice, from the north frieze. Acropolis Museum, Athens.

---

maintained that any single rule or point of view capable of being easily expressed in language could, in the sphere of religion, hold good for all men at all ages and at all times, unless it were some apparently straightforward, but in fact appallingly complicated precept or maxim, such as 'Know yourself' or 'Evil will breed evil'.

In the legends of Greece there are very many examples of the variety, the depth, the simplicity, and to our minds, perhaps, the inconsistency of religious experience. One need go no farther than the walls of the Acropolis at Athens where, near the theatre of Herodes Atticus, there used once to be, they say, the tomb of the hero Hippolytus, the loved and illegitimate son of the great King Theseus, founder of Attica, whose own temple stands below the walls of the citadel. In Greece no symbol is ever adequate; yet when I look at the heads and bodies of ephebes, made from marble and from real life, the story of Hippolytus will often come to mind. It is a story which can at least illustrate, if not explain, the depth, the contrariety and the purity of Greek religious feeling in the classical period.

Hippolytus, son of the Queen of the Amazons and of the great King of Athens, was devoted to the virgin goddess Artemis. His life was spent in hunting, riding and athletic sports in the company of other young men and he was so much the favourite of Artemis that he was actually privileged to feel her presence and to hear her voice. He was upright, blameless, enjoying the love of his father and of his fellow citizens, admired by all for his noble qualities. Yet there was something wrong. In our terminology we might say that he was not 'adjusted to reality'. The Greeks said that he aroused the jealousy of the

Head of the EPHEBE OF MARATHON. Bronze, 4th century. Found in the sea near Marathon, 1925. National Museum, Athens.
(Page 76) STELE OF AN ARMED RUNNER, representing him either at the moment of arrival at his goal or of collapse. Parian marble, 3 ft. 4⅛ in. high. Attic. Date, about 520 B.C. Found near the Theseum in 1902. National Museum, Athens.
(Page 77) BURIAL STELE OF AN EPHEBE, found in Salamis. Marble, 3 ft. 7¼ in. high. The youth with a cloak, holding a bird in his left hand, is raising his right hand to a bird-cage; on a pillar, a cat; in front, the small servant and friend of the dead man. Attic. Date, towards the end of the 5th century; reminiscent of the Parthenon frieze. National Museum, Athens.

goddess Aphrodite. For Hippolytus was not interested in women or in physical love; his whole devotion was to manly exercises and to the pure company of the goddess Artemis. These exalted tastes were enough to destroy him. Aphrodite, angry to find her altars neglected, was determined to revenge herself upon the young man. She forced his step-mother, Phaedra, to fall in love with him and it was useless for Phaedra, in the grip of the goddess, to struggle against a passion that was divinely inspired. In the end she was compelled to let her feelings be revealed to Hippolytus, who was shocked and horrified beyond words. Phaedra then hanged herself, but to preserve what she still thought of as her 'good name' she left a message behind for her husband in which she stated that her suicide had been caused by the wicked advances made to her by Hippolytus. Theseus believed the story and cursed his son, invoking his own father, Poseidon, to carry out the vengeance which he desired. So, through the intervention of Poseidon, Hippolytus was hurled from his chariot and his bruised body was dragged along the rocky ground by his own horses. Before he died, he was brought into the presence of his father, and at this point, in the version of the story given to us by Euripides, the goddess Artemis appears, explains how guiltless was the young man, how foolishly credulous was Theseus, and how the whole tragedy was brought about by the jealous anger of a rival goddess. Artemis states that, much as she loves Hippolytus, she could not have saved him. She says:

> 'There is a rule among the gods—
> That none of us will check another god's desire
> When it is shown. Instead we always stand aside.'

The best that she can do is to get even with Aphrodite at a later date, when, in the fullness of time, she will see to it that Aphrodite's favourite amongst men, Adonis, is destroyed. And Hippolytus himself, though nothing can save him, will, after his death, be worshipped as a hero. Meanwhile he is reconciled with his father and he dies in a kind of peace.

Detail from the BURIAL STELE OF PANAETIUS, found in the Ceramicus at Athens. Memorial to a rider (cf. page 83). Here a boy with a hoop is depicted on a *lekythos*. Attic. Date, second half of 5th century. National Museum, Athens.

There are many such stories in Greek mythology, and they all show a view of the divine that differs very widely from the views held by Christians or by Jews. Certainly in the story of Hippolytus it must seem shocking to us that a good man is killed for no good reason and to find that, if there is a reason, it amounts, in a way, almost to a kind of petty jealousy felt by a divine power. Yet when we think along these lines we may be thinking, in our own way, more anthropomorphically than ever did the Greeks. For to them Aphrodite was more than a statue. She was a fierce power, and a power incompatible with much else that is valuable in life. Artemis too was jealous of her own and could inspire a passionate devotion. Between these and other conflicting forces what man can claim any security? Even the wise and enduring Odysseus, the favourite of Athena, is harried throughout his days by the vengeful anger of the god of the sea. Indeed it is easier for a Jew or a Christian than for a Greek to make his peace, or to believe that he has made it, with the powers that govern the universe.

Hippolytus himself, at the beginning of Euripides' play, little knowing the fate in store for him, is confident in his manliness, his virtue and in the protec-tion of his chosen goddess. As he comes in from his hunting he lays a garland by the statue of Artemis in front of his father's palace and speaks the following words:

'For you, my lady, I have made and bring to you
This wreath of twined flowers from a virgin meadow,
A place where shepherd never thought to feed his flocks
Nor ever came the stroke of iron. Instead the bees
Cross and recross this virgin meadow in the spring,
And native Shame waters the ground with river dew,
And from his garden only those may pluck the flowers
Who were elect from birth by a wise purity
In all things, and never had to learn it. Evil men
Have no right there. And so, dear lady, take from this
Reverent hand a binding for your golden hair.
For I alone of men am so distinguished as to be
Constantly with you and to speak and hear your words.
I hear the voice, but I have never seen your face.
O, let me end my life as I have started it!'

In this speech there is certainly an element of pride, but there is also a deep humility and a deep religious feeling. And at the very end of the play we shall also find a strange religious sense conveyed to us by the dramatist who, both in his own times and in ours, has been either praised or attacked for his rationalism. When Hippolytus, dying in agony, is carried in to his father's presence, Theseus has already been informed by the goddess Artemis of the cruel mistake which he has made. Artemis is still present when the wounded youth is brought in by his attendants, and the following scene takes place:

ARTEMIS

Poor youth, how you are yoked together with your pain!
It was the goodness of your heart destroyed your life.

HIPPOLYTUS

Ha!
O heavenly breath of fragrance! Even in my pains
I feel your presence, and my body grows more light.
Is Artemis, the goddess, present in this place?

ARTEMIS

Poor youth, she is, and loves you more than all the gods.

HIPPOLYTUS

You see me, lady, and my state, my wretched state?

ARTEMIS

I see you, but my eyes are not allowed to weep.

HIPPOLYTUS

No more the huntsman for you and the serving man. . . .

ARTEMIS

No more. Yet in your dying you are dear to me.

HIPPOLYTUS

No more to guard your statues or to drive your steeds.

ARTEMIS

No. It was cruel Cypris wished these things to be.

HIPPOLYTUS

Alas! I recognize the god who took my life.

ARTEMIS

Jealous of honour, angry at your living pure.

HIPPOLYTUS

Alone, I see, she has destroyed all three of us.

ARTEMIS

Yes. You, your father, and his wife, the third of you.

HIPPOLYTUS

Then I must weep too for my father's sufferings.

ARTEMIS

It was the counsel of a god deceived his mind.

HIPPOLYTUS

Unhappy father in this suffering of yours!

THESEUS

My son, I am destroyed and have no joy in life.

HIPPOLYTUS

More than myself, I grieve for you and your mistake.

Detail from the BURIAL STELE OF PANAETIUS, found in the Ceramicus at Athens. Memorial to a rider (cf. page 76). The dead youth is represented on a vessel (*lutrophoros*), leaning on his spear as he bids farewell to his father. Attic. Date, second half of 5th century. National Museum, Athens.

THESEUS

I wish that I, my child, could die instead of you.

HIPPOLYTUS

Bitter the gifts your sire, Poseidon, gave to you.

THESEUS

I wish that it had never mounted to my lips.

HIPPOLYTUS

Why so? You would have killed me, angry as you were.

THESEUS

Yes, for the gods had cheated me of my good sense.

HIPPOLYTUS

Alas!
I wish the race of men had power to curse the gods.

ARTEMIS

Be satisfied. For no, not in the dark of earth
Shall I allow, at Cypris' pleasure, rage to light
Upon your body unavenged; and this because
Of your god-fearingness and of your noble mind.
For I shall take from her with my own hand the one
Of mortals whom above all others she loves best,
And so with my unerring bow become avenged.
And now on you, unhappy one, for all your pains
I shall bestow the greatest honours in this land
Of Troizen. For unmarried girls, before they wed,
Shall cut their hair to do you honour. You will have
For ages long the harvest of their mourning tears.

BURIAL STELE OF MYNNO, seated on a chair, spinning. Found between Athens and Piraeus. Pentelic marble. Height, just under 2 ft. Attic. Date, the last third of the 5th century. Altes Museum, Berlin.

And always among maidens there will be desire
To make their songs of you. It will not pass away
Or nameless sink to silence, Phaedra's love for you.
And you, O child of aged Aigeus, I bid take
Your son up in your arms and give him your embrace.
It was against your will you slew him, and it is
Natural for men to err when gods point out the way.
And you, Hippolytus, I counsel not to hate
Your father, for you know the fate by which you died.
Farewell! For I am not allowed to see the dead,
Or stain my eye with the last gasps of dying men,
And you I see already near that evil thing.

HIPPOLYTUS

O farewell, blessed maiden, go upon your way
Easily now you leave our long companionship.
I end my quarrel with my father, as you bid,
And as in old times also I obeyed your words.

There are many other stories—those of Orpheus and Adonis, for example
—where a favourite of the gods is killed through the action of some other
divinity and is afterwards himself raised either to the divine or the heroic level.
And it is neither impious nor fanciful to suggest that these stories of the
young man killed and in some strange way afterwards invested with new life
have left their mark on the religious ceremonies which to this day are celebrated in Greece at Easter. This, however, is an aspect of Greek religion which
can more conveniently be considered in connexion with the Mysteries. Here,
when one is thinking of the story of Hippolytus as given to us by Euripides,
other reflexions come to mind. It is clear that both the author of the play and
the audience who, just after the death of Pericles, awarded it first prize in the
dramatic contest, must have held a view of life which differs considerably from
that of the monotheistic religions. They accepted a situation where a young
man, renowned for his purity and his godfearingness, is, for that reason,
exposed to the greatest dangers and is finally destroyed. Not only do the gods
war against each other, but, to put it from an ordinary human standpoint, the
gods behave badly. Euripides himself realizes this and no doubt the 'advanced'

86

intellectual elements in the audience would have applauded such lines as that put into the mouth of one of Hippolytus' attendants who says:

'Gods should be wiser and more moderate than men.'

But the fact is that in the story, and by ordinary human standards, they are not. Yet they should be dutifully worshipped and they are the right objects of men's affections. Men themselves, however careful they may be, live in a state of very great insecurity. They are poised between a number of tremendous and conflicting forces. Even a conspicuously prudent man like Odysseus, the favourite of Athena, cannot escape the wrath of Poseidon. Sins are often, as in the case of Oedipus, entirely accidental, but are still visited by the most dreadful punishments.

We should be unwise, I think, to consider those who held such beliefs as either spiritually or intellectually slavish. A puritan or a rationalist may say 'If your god is not as good and as consistent as I am, then your god does not deserve my worship'; but such a speaker will be ignorant of the arrogance of his presuppositions. Certainly to the Greeks such arrogance seems to have been the one sin which inevitably led to ruin. No people in history has been better capable of rational thought and of the orderly arrangement of human affairs: no people has been more conscious of the final inadequacy of both the one and the other. It was necessary (indeed life and sanity might depend on it) to recognize the existence and the power of forces not perfectly understood.

Such reflexions as these have occurred often to me as I have contemplated the landscape of Greece or looked at the expressions in the faces of the sculptured heads of ephebes.

THERE IS a legend that Asclepius, the great healer and son of Apollo by a mortal woman, used his skill to bring Hippolytus to life, and for this act of impiety was killed by a thunderbolt of Zeus. However this may be, Asclepius himself, like Heracles, after all his sufferings, joined the circle of the gods and was able to appear in later times to his worshippers. But, in mythology, he was about the last to be so elevated. Menelaus, it is true, was promised a release from death and a happy future in an earthly paradise. But he was the husband of Helen, and regarded by the gods as the son-in-law of Zeus. In general it may be said that in the generation before the Trojan war, direct intercourse between gods and men, the intercourse of marriage, rape, apotheosis or even the sharing of meals together, abruptly ceased. Man was left on his own and, at least according to Homer, if he survived death at all, it was as a thin, unhappy and squeaking ghost.

Yet there were other beliefs, not part of, or only loosely attached to, the heroic tradition, which could console the ordinary man, and which have left their mark both on sculpture and on literature. They are beliefs about which it is extremely difficult to dogmatize. Our knowledge of them is small and there is some inconsistency in the knowledge that we do possess. It is evident, for instance, that those who were initiated in the Mysteries of Eleusis did feel that they were guaranteed a better life in the world after death than would be the lot of the uninitiated. In the *Frogs* of Aristophanes we find that Elysium, the earthly paradise promised to Menelaus, is now located in the world below, beyond the area where the great sinners have their eternal punishment. In fact the mythological scene of Plato, Virgil and Dante is already almost fixed. We know too that to the average Athenian the mysteries were so important that on the mere suspicion that Alcibiades and his friends had taken part in some kind of a private charade in which the ceremonies of Eleusis were made fun of, the whole State was thrown into confusion, and Alcibiades was deprived

BURIAL STELE OF A WOMAN. Detail, showing head of the deceased, who is handing a jewel-box to a servant. Found in Piraeus. Attic. Date, early 4th century. National Museum, Athens.

of his command in Sicily and exiled—the result of which was, in all probability, that Athens lost the war and the empire of the Mediterranean. On the
other hand one should remember that in Thucydides there is no mention at
all of an after life, though there are several points in his narrative where, if the
idea of such a thing had been in the thoughts of his characters, it might
appropriately have been introduced. And though Plato makes Socrates argue
for immortality, he is evidently much concerned with the difficulty of convincing even the nearest and dearest of his disciples. Moreover, there is a sense
in which the immortality promised or suggested by Plato is of a very rarefied
and exclusive kind. In fact it appears to be limited to philosophers. Then, if
one looks at the evidence of inscriptions, it appears that the only class of people
who are promised immortality at all are those who by dying in battle or
performing some great work will be remembered after their death. There is no
reference to any individual survival. The only form of immortality recognized
is the immortality of fame. And in the beautiful reliefs on grave-stones it is
the past life lived on earth and a kind of serenity in accepting the inevitable
which are so nobly expressed; there is no hint of anything in the future on
which heart, imagination or belief may be set.

Here again one is faced with contradictions. Grave-stones and the inscriptions upon them are, of course, conventional things. Not all of those who
have caused to be inscribed in our own churchyards sentences expressing a
certain hope of reunion with their loved ones in another world have been so
convinced of this prospect as their words declare. And in ancient Greek
religion there was certainly no dogma on the exact organization of the future
life. It may be, therefore, that Greek pessimism on the subject was as conventional as some of our optimism, and that there were many feelings and ideas
which never found their way into the epitaphs of poets or into the funereal
sculptures. It may be that life was viewed in so vivid a light, that the enquiring
eye faltered when it tried to look beyond the shadow of death, where the clear

BURIAL STELE OF TIMARISTA AND CRITO, found in Camiros on Rhodes
in 1930. White marble. Height of the stele 5 ft. 4 in. The elder woman, probably the
mother (according to the inscription, Timarista), is placing her right hand around the neck
of the younger (Crito), who is approaching her with her right hand raised. Opinions differ
about style (Attic or Ionic). Date, about 460. Museum, Rhodes.

lines are lost and where imagination or abstract thought has to take the place of vision. So, with nothing clear or certain to be discovered, there was nothing to be brought back and incorporated in works of art or literature which were designed to appeal immediately to the mind. There were only symbols, and Plato, in his 'myths', is the only classical writer who deliberately and for his own intellectual ends makes use of them.

We do know, however, for certain that the ordinary man (if such a phrase can be used of the Greeks) did entertain other ideas whether together with or in contradiction to the conventional pessimism or agnosticism with regard to a future life. The cult of Demeter and Persephone at Eleusis had existed long before Athens became a great power and the mysteries taught or shown there may have been of a very ancient origin. The place had been of some importance even in Mycenean times and there is some evidence for supposing that the rites were imported from Crete. When Eleusis was brought into the political structure of Attica, the mysteries were taken over, in a sense, by Athens, though the two priestly families of Eleusis, the Eumolpidae and the Keryces, preserved a special position in the guardianship and administration of the rites.

The story of Demeter and Persephone is well known. Demeter is the goddess of the surface of the earth, with its corn and its fruit trees; but she is connected with Pluto, 'the rich', the god of the earth's interior, where the corn grows in darkness before it shoots up in the spring; and Pluto is also the Lord of the Dead. Demeter's daughter Persephone remains with him during the dark months when the seed corn is underground and then, at the right time, rejoins her mother in the light of the sun. Commenting on this myth, Professor Guthrie writes as follows:

'Out of this association there arose at Eleusis the belief that Demeter had in her gift not only the fertility of the land, but immortality for the human soul. Did the minds of her worshippers work in the same way as that of the Evangelist: "Except a corn of wheat fall into the ground and die, it abideth alone: but if it die, it bringeth forth much fruit," and of St Paul: "That which thou sowest is not quickened, except it die"? Did they draw the analogy that just as the dried-up grain by being buried in the earth sprang into new life, so when the dead are buried they may find a source of new life too? It is rash to dogmatize about the processes of thought of unselfconscious people, and we may rest content with the known fact that the goddess of fertility was also for them the giver of immortality.' (W. K. C. Guthrie. *The Greeks and their Gods.*)

We know, from Aristophanes' *Frogs* and from other sources, quite a lot about the preliminary stages of the festival at Eleusis as it was held in the fifth century B.C. It was only with regard to the final act of 'Beholding' that lips were religiously sealed. The fact that this solemn ceremony could also be the occasion for much merriment is worth noting. The procession itself and some of its religious and secular aspects are well described by Professor Guthrie.

'Not only new rites, but a new god, arose from the connexion of the mysteries with Athens. This was Iacchos. To cover the distance from Athens to Eleusis a procession was formed and passed along what came to be known as the Sacred Way between the two towns with dancing, singing and joyful shouts of "Iacche, iacche!" From this, by the personification which came so readily to the Greek mind, arose the idea of a god of the joyful cry, and who was he likely to be but Dionysus, himself the patron of wild dancing and already known as "Euius" from the ecstatic cry "Euoi" that was uttered by his impassioned worshippers? The cry was now regarded as an invocation to Iacchos, and Iacchos identified with Dionysus, with whose dress and attributes his image was adorned. This image, as well as the sacred emblems from the *Eleusinion*, was borne from his temple to the gathering point of the procession in the market place, and thence carried the whole way to Eleusis, like the saint and relics of many a Mediterranean procession today. The invocation of Iacchos has a prominent place in the *Frogs*, as also has another incident which offered obvious scope for the parodist, namely a proclamation that was made before the start of the procession bidding all stand aside who were impure, unprepared by the proper preliminary rites or in any other way unfitted to take part. One of these preliminary rites was purification by bathing in the sea, for which all candidates for initiation went down to the coast close to Athens on an appointed day. The procession took more than one day to cover the twelve miles of road, for it had to halt for all sorts of performances by the way. Later Greek writers mention dances, sacrifices, libations and hymns. The way was lined with the shrines of gods and heroes, each of whom must have his due. Thus torchlight played its part in adding to the atmosphere of excitement. At a certain bridge across the river Kephissos, a curious practice was observed that must have far antedated the days of the procession and been incorporated in it. As the procession arrived, one of its number sitting on the bridge, and answered possibly by the others, hurled abuse and curses, as one authority says, "at the most distinguished of the citizens". This "bridgery" (gephyrismos), as the often obscene jesting and cursing came to be called from the scene of its enact-ment, was not confined to the Eleusian procession nor to the Kephissos bridge. Pointless as it sounds, there are parallels from Mediterranean custom to suggest that it had a practical aim, being considered effective in averting the evil eye.

'We need not waste time in speculating on the nature of the final spectacle in the actual telesterion at Eleusis. This it was that admitted a man to the highest grade of initiation, that of *Epoptes*, Beholder. Of these last solemn rites it was not permitted to speak. "A great awe of the gods holds back the voice" as the Homeric Hymn puts it, and a chorus of Sophocles says that a golden key is laid upon the tongue of mortals by the Eumolpid priests. The secret was well kept. Christian writers, in their attacks on pagan ceremonies, have claimed to know and to reveal it, but we may well be chary of accepting their late and hostile accounts as evidence for what went on at Eleusis in the fifth or fourth century B.C. We know however that it consisted of a revelation or spectacle, even if there is doubt as to the precise nature of the things revealed. All evidence leads to the conclusion that the effect was achieved by immediate action upon the senses. The initiate was shown things, and convinced of his salvation by the evidence of his own eyes. The climax was called the beholding and the chief officiating priest the hierophant, which means literally a show-man of holy things. He was not a teacher. As Aristotle said, the initiate was not required to learn anything, but rather after suitable preparation to undergo an experience and be put in a certain state. One can scarcely speak of anything so definite as doctrine in connexion with Eleusis. The root idea was more akin

---

DEDICATORY RELIEF FROM ELEUSIS, found in 1859. In the centre is the youth Triptolemus. Demeter stands in front of him, holding a sceptre and offering him ears of corn. On the right, the daughter of Demeter, Persephone, or Kore, holding a torch in her left hand, is placing a garland on Triptolemus' head. Pentelic marble. Height 7 ft. 2½ in. Attic. Date, about 450–440 B.C.

to magic, whose efficacy depends on the thoroughness of the preparatory measures and the punctilious correctness with which certain prescribed actions are carried out. Clearly also a large part was played by the emotional state which had been induced by the series of preliminary actions leading to the ultimate revelation set, as it appears, in a scene of contrasts between darkness and the dazzling light of hundreds of torches. It may be doubted however whether Dikaiopolis and his friends were so easily overawed as some. The Athenian loved a show, and had no wish to water down the impressive and spectacular elements of the mysteries; indeed he added to them. But one cannot help feeling that it remained to him primarily a show, with certain desirable consequences. "Worshipful daughter of Demeter, what a grand smell of roast pork!" is how the slave Xanthias (in the *Frogs*) interrupts the solemn invocation of Iacchos, and Dionysos' only rebuke is, "Well, keep quiet and you may get a bit of the offal." Another reference to the preliminary sacrifice of pigs also illustrates the severely practical mentality of the Athenian. Trygaios, the Athenian farmer who is the hero of the *Peace*, is told by Hermes that he has committed a crime against the gods for which the only possible punishment is death, and replies imperturbably: "Then lend me three drachmas to buy a pig—I must get initiated before I die."' (W. K. C. Guthrie. *The Greeks and their Gods.*)

DEDICATORY RELIEF to Hermes and the Nymphs from PHALERON. Found in 1893. Marble, 2 ft. 7 in. high. On the side shown (top): Echilos carries off Basile; the galloping horses of the quadriga are driven by Hermes. Attic. Date, about 400. National Museum, Athens. *Below:* ELEUSIS, view over the remains of the temple.

THE MARBLES OF AEGINA

VISIBLE from the whole coast-line of Athens and Piraeus, and from any high ground in the city itself is the conical shape of the island of Aegina. In ancient times this island was a naval power capable of disputing the mastership of the sea first with Samos and then with Athens. The silver 'tortoises' of Aegina were the first Greek coins and formed a respectable standard of currency for many years. The people of Aegina played a distinguished part in the battles of the Persian invasion under Xerxes, though at the time of Marathon, when the Persian forces were directed only against Athens, they held aloof and would no doubt have been glad to have seen their dangerous rival destroyed. It was primarily in order to attack Aegina that Athens built the fleet that won freedom for the whole of Greece at Salamis. In 459 B.C., some twenty years after Salamis, Aegina was decisively defeated by the Athenians and the island was brought into the Athenian empire. But the Dorian people of the island resented the loss of their old glory and independence. They and the Corinthians were most active in impelling Sparta to enter upon the long and ruinous Peloponnesian War, and they were some of the first people to suffer from it. The Athenians banished them from their island and resettled it with colonists of their own, including the families of Aristophanes and of Plato. After the defeat of Athens, the Aeginetans were restored; but the great days were over.

Before the Athenian conquest the Aeginetans built the great temple for Aphaia, a virgin goddess who has been identified with the Cretan Britomartis. This Britomartis (which means 'sweet maid' in Cretan) was wooed by Minos and to avoid his advances threw herself from a cliff into the sea from which she was rescued by the fishermen, taking the name Dictynna from the Greek word for 'net'. She then escaped to Aegina. Very much later she appears as a kind of female Sir Galahad and is the heroine of the Third Book of *The Faerie Queene*, 'contayning the Legend of Britomartis or of Chastitie'.

AEGINA. The Temple of Aphaia (formerly known as the Temple of Panhellenian Zeus or of Athena). Doric periptery of yellowish limestone (Poros), ornamented with Parian marble. The figures from the pediments, now in Munich, date from about 510–480 B.C., the earliest being those of the west pediment.

The sculptures from the pediments of her temple were unearthed in 1811. A vivid account of this operation is given in the journal of C. R. Cockerell, who well describes the period of the great depredations, when Greece was still under Turkish domination.

Cockerell, an enthusiastic student of architecture, had left England in 1810 just before his twenty-third birthday. He met Byron in Athens and found him on the point of sailing for Malta in 'the transport which is carrying Lord Elgin's marbles'. Cockerell and his friends, leaving Piraeus for Aegina at night, overtook the ship that was carrying Lord Byron.

'Passing under the stern we sang a favourite song of his, on which he looked out of the windows and invited us in. There we drank a glass of port with him, Colonel Travers, and two of the English officers, and talked of the three English frigates that had attacked five Turkish ones and a sloop of war off Corfu, and had taken and burnt three of them.'

After saying good-bye to Byron, the party went on to Aegina. Cockerell's description of the scene and of his discoveries is as follows:

'The seas hereabouts are still infested with pirates, as they always have been. One of the workmen pointed me out the pirate boats off Sunium, which is one of their favourite haunts, and which can be seen from the temple platform. But they never molested us during the twenty days and nights we camped out there, for our party, with servants and janissary, was too strong to be meddled with. We got our provisions and labourers from the town, our fuel was the wild thyme, there were abundance of partridges to eat, and we bought kids from the shepherds, and when work was over for the day, there was a grand roasting of them over a blazing fire with an accompaniment of native music, singing and dancing. On the platform was growing a crop of barley, but on the actual ruins and fallen fragments of the temple itself no great amount of vegetable earth had collected, so that without very much labour we were able to find and examine all the stones necessary for a complete architectural

AEGINA. TEMPLE OF APHAIA. The two-storied inner rows of columns reconstructed in 1956.

analysis and restoration. At the end of a few days we had learnt all we could wish to know of the construction, from the stylobate to the tiles, and had done all we came to do.

'But meanwhile a startling incident had occurred which wrought us all to the highest pitch of excitement. On the second day one of the excavators, working in the interior portico, struck on a piece of Parian marble which, as the building itself is of stone, arrested his attention. It turned out to be the head of a helmeted warrior, perfect in every feature. It lay with the face turned upwards, and as the features came out by degrees you can imagine nothing like the state of rapture and excitement to which we were wrought. Here was an altogether new interest, which set us to work with a will. Soon another head was turned up, then a leg and a foot, and finally, to make a long story short, we found under the fallen portions of the tympanum and the cornice of the eastern and western pediments no less than sixteen statues and thirteen heads, legs, arms, etc.

'It was not to be expected that we should be allowed to carry away what we had found without opposition. However much people may neglect their own possessions, as soon as they see them coveted by others they begin to value them. The primates of the island came to us in a body and read a state-ment made by the council of the island in which they begged us to desist from our operations, for that heaven only knew what misfortunes might not fall on the island in general, and the immediately surrounding land in particular, if we continued them. Such a rubbishy pretence of superstitious fear was obviously a mere excuse to extort money, and as we felt that it was only fair that we should pay, we sent our drago-man with them to the village to treat about the sum; and meanwhile a boat which we had ordered from Athens having arrived, we embarked the marbles without delay and sent them off under the care of Foster and Linckh, with the janissary, to the Piraeus, and from thence they were carried up to Athens by night to avoid exciting attention. Haller and I remained to carry on the digging, which we did with all possible vigour. The marbles being gone, the primates came to be easier to deal with. We completed our bargain with them to pay them 800 piastres,

AEGINA. FIGURE FROM THE EAST PEDIMENT OF THE TEMPLE OF ALPHAEA: Head of Heracles.

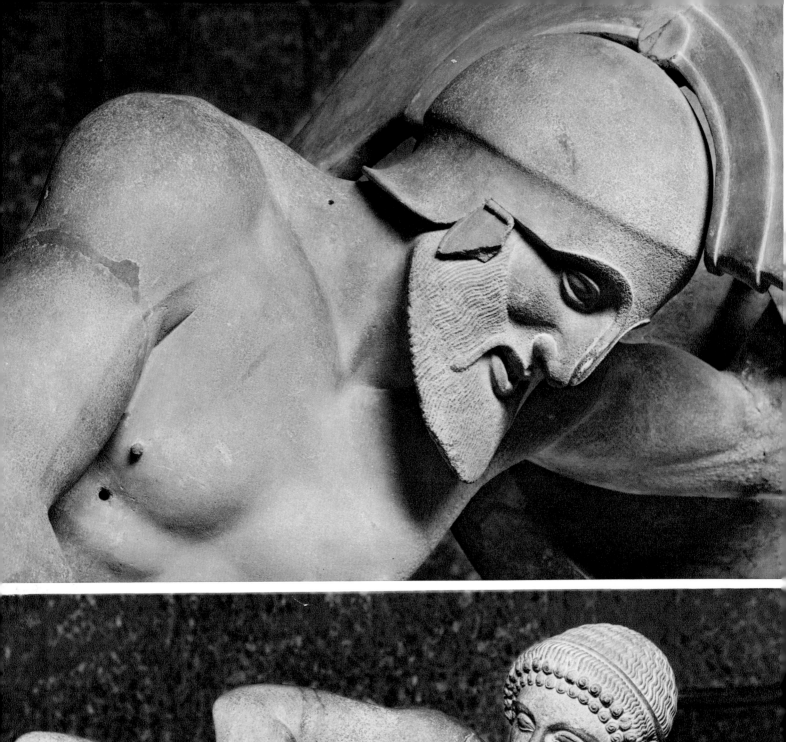

about 40 l., for the antiquities we had found, with leave to continue the digging till we had explored the whole site.' (*Travels in Southern Europe and the Levant, 1810-1817, the Journal of C. R. Cockerell, R.A.*, edited by his son S. P. Cockerell.)

Cockerell himself did all he could to see that the marbles were purchased by the British Museum. The French Government and Prince Louis of Bavaria, however, were also in the field. Nevertheless it seems certain that the marbles would have joined the sculptures from the Parthenon in London, if it had not been for the fact that the representative of the British Museum, who had travelled out to Malta, was, whether by accident or by the design of other interested parties, misinformed as to the place and date of the sale. He failed to put in an appearance at Xante on the right date, and, much to Cockerell's disgust, the Aegina marbles were bought by the agent of the Prince of Bavaria for 10,000 sequins.

AEGINA. FIGURES FROM THE PEDIMENTS OF THE ALPHAEA. They represent the battles of the ancestors of the Aeginetans at Troy. *Above:* Dying warrior, from the east pediment. *Below:* Wounded warrior, from the west pediment. Glyptothek, Munich.

DELOS

THE SMALL island of Delos, in the centre of the Cyclades, was said to have been the birth-place of Apollo. In early times it was the great meeting place of the Ionians, who came to worship Apollo and to delight him with songs, dances and games. In some of the legends it is said that the island miraculously appeared from the surface of the sea to afford a refuge to Leto in her time of travail, all other parts of the earth having refused to give her sanctuary, since she was to bear the children of Zeus, Apollo and Artemis, and the jealous wife of Zeus, Hera, would visit her vengeance on any land that gave succour to one who had, at least for a time, supplanted her in her husband's affections.

The story as told in the Homeric Hymn to Delian Apollo is more dignified. 'Shall I sing', the poet says, in his address to Apollo, 'of how at first Leto gave birth to you, a joy to men, leaning herself against Mount Cynthus in a rocky island, in Delos washed by water, and on both sides a dark wave beneath the shrill-breathing winds came onwards towards the shore?'

The poet goes on to describe how none of the other islands would dare to receive so great a god. Delos, however, was a poor island and Leto, in asking the island for its sanctuary, points out that, though it can never hope to be prosperous in agriculture or in the breeding of animals, it is likely to do very well in the future, when people will come from all sides to bring their offerings to the temple which will be built to her son. The island is pleased by this promise, but is still not entirely reassured. It speaks to Leto and says:

'All the same, Leto, there is this saying which I am afraid of, and I will not hide it from you. They say that Apollo is going to be one who is very

---

Above: NAXOS HARBOUR. The entrance to the capital (both in former times and today) of the island of the same name. On the small projecting isle of Palati are the remains of an ancient doorway of the temple of Dionysus. *Below:* DELOS (modern Greek, *Mikra Dili*), sacred precinct of Apollo.
(Page 108) DELOS. The town and harbour seen from Cynthus.
(Page 109) DELOS. One of the lions of the Sacred Way. Naxian marble. Date, 6th century B.C.

arrogant, one who will be very much in the first place among the gods and among mortal men on the fruitful earth. So I am terribly afraid in my mind and in my heart that when he first sees the light of the sun, he will despise this island—and it is true that my soil is very rocky—and will overturn me and push me down with his feet into the depths of the sea. And then a great wave of the salt sea will wash over my head for ever, and he will come to some other land which will please him, and in it make his temple and his woody groves. And as for me, the octopuses will have their lairs in me and the black seals will make their dwellings undisturbed, because I shall have no people.'

Leto reassures the island and swears that here, and nowhere else, shall be the sanctuary of Apollo, who will honour Delos above all places.

And so while the earth laughed for joy, Apollo was born. His mother did not feed him from her breast. Instead he was given nectar and ambrosia. 'And Leto was glad, because she had borne an archer and a strong son.' As for Apollo, no sooner had he tasted the divine food than it was found impossible to confine him in the golden cords or bands which the goddesses, his nurses, had put round him. He spoke out immediately and said: 'The lyre shall be dear to me and the curved bow, and I will reveal to men the unerring will of Zeus.' At once he began to stride over the earth and all the immortal goddesses were amazed at him.

The poet goes on to say that, though there are many other temples to the god, it is still in Delos that Apollo most delights.

'There the Ionians with their trailing robes gather together, with their children and their modest wives. And with their thoughts on you, they delight you with boxing and dancing and singing, when they hold their contests. Any man would say that they were immortal and ageless for ever, if he were to come upon them at this time, when the Ionians are all gathered together. For

---

Above: CORINTH. THE TEMPLE OF APOLLO, a Doric periptery, of which seven columns, 23 ft. 7½ in. high, made of porous limestone, are still standing. The compact shape of the monolithic columns, each with twenty flutings, seems to indicate that the temple was built in the first half of the 6th century. *Below:* NEMEA. TEMPLE OF ZEUS. Doric. Middle of 4th century.

---

he would see the grace in each one of them and it would delight his heart to look at the men and the fine-girdled women, and their swift ships and all their wealth.'

Then too there are the girls of Delos, the priestesses of Apollo. They are 'a great wonder', for they not only sing songs of praise to Apollo, Artemis and Leto, but can also sing of 'the men and women of the past' and they can imitate the dialects of people from all over the world. It is to these girls that the blind poet addresses himself last.

'Farewell, all of you,' he says, 'but remember me in the future when any man of those on earth, some stranger who has been far and wide, comes here and asks you: "Maidens, who do you think is the sweetest of the singers that come here? In whom do you most delight?" Then you must all answer together and, with one voice, tell him "It is a blind man, and he lives in rocky Chios."'

On the whole the goddess Leto kept her promise to the island and it enjoyed long periods of prosperity, though, as we shall see, there were some inconveniences. As the great meeting place of the Ionians it was natural that Delos should be chosen as the centre of the Athenian-led confederacy that came into being after the retreat of the Persians from Greece in 478 B.C. Later the treasury of the League was moved to Athens, and Delos, though it did not pay tribute like the other allies, came under Athenian control. The

---

MYCENAE in Argos, described by Homer as the 'well-built' seat of Agamemnon, 'rich in gold', built according to legend by Perseus, explored by Schliemann as the centre of the so-called Creto-Mycenaean culture. *Above:* View inside the fortifications at the bottom of the hill on which the citadel stands. In the centre is the circular Royal Burial Place where, during Schliemann's excavations (1876-7), were found seventeen bodies and the gold treasure which is now in Athens. At first held to be the tombs of Agamemnon and his family mentioned by Pausanias, but perhaps more than 400 years older. *Below:* THE LION GATE stands at the end of an entrance-way 33 ft. wide and 49 ft. long at the north-west corner of the stronghold. The doorway is 10 ft. 8 in. high; the lintel stone is over 16 ft. long, 3 ft. 4 in. thick and 8 ft. 2½ in. wide. Above this is a block of brownish-grey limestone, 9 ft. 10 in. high, which carries the lion relief.

Athenians seem constantly to have been worried about preserving the sanctity of the place and their religious scruples must have caused the Delians themselves considerable annoyance. The island had already been 'purified' once by Pisistratus, but it was 'purified' twice again during the Peloponnesian War. On the first of these occasions all graves were dug up (providing for Thucydides archaeological evidence that the original inhabitants had been Carians) and for the future no one was allowed either to die or give birth to a child on the island. Those who felt the necessity for either birth or death had to go immediately to the adjacent island of Rhenia. The Athenians were not even satisfied with this, but later expelled the Delians from their homes—we do not know for how long a time.

In later years, after the final collapse of Athenian sea power, Delos, while retaining its importance as a place of worship, grew wealthy as the centre of the corn trade in the Aegean. But when Rome came upon the scene the Delians unwisely allied themselves with King Perseus of Macedon. Athens had allied herself with Rome and, after the Romans had dealt with Perseus, they rewarded Athens by putting the island into her hands. Once more, now in 166 B.C., the Athenians removed the wretched Delians and populated Delos with colonists of her own. About a hundred years later Delos was sacked by the pirates against whom Pompey was shortly to organize his celebrated campaign and the inhabitants, who had for some time been doing very well out of the traffic in slaves, were sold into slavery themselves. From this disaster Delos appears never fully to have recovered.

HEAD OF A YOUTH. Bronze. Exceptionally well preserved. The paste inlay of the eyes is missing. Region where found unknown. Doric. Date, about 460 B.C. Antiquarium, Berlin.

MYCENAE AND THE HOUSE OF ATREUS

ABOUT nine miles from the sea, in a fold of the mountains that look down upon the fertile plain of Argos, stands the sombre, powerful and immensely impressive citadel of 'golden Mycenae', the palace of the Atridae and the fortress that controlled the routes from the Gulf of Argos to Corinth and the north. It was first inhabited (3000–2800 B.C.) by a pre-Hellenic people, possibly the same as the 'Carians' whose graves were unearthed at Delos. In the period of about 2000–1600 B.C. the place fell into the hands, so the archaeologists say, of some of the first invaders of a Greek-speaking race. The circle of graves inside the Lion Gate, which were excavated by Schliemann in 1876, belong to this period, as do all but the finest of the beehive tombs. But it was in the final period (1400–1150 B.C.) that the massive fortifications were built, together with the Lion Gate and the vast 'Treasury of Atreus'. At this time, the time just before the Trojan War, Mycenae was without doubt a place of quite exceptional power, riches and importance. At the end of this period the town and palaces were destroyed by fire, either as the result of the Dorian invasion or of a raid from overseas. Though the town was inhabited again it never regained its importance.

It is not only over archaeologists that this place has exercised and continues to exercise an extraordinary and uncanny fascination. 'Here', as the Tutor says to Orestes at the beginning of Sophocles' *Electra*, 'is the house of the children of Pelops, a house of death and destruction.' No family has left such enduring marks in literature and in mythology. Their history is a long chain of evil, interrupted from time to time by appalling catastrophe. No one who has visited Mycenae will dispute the fact that this powerful rock set among the mountains is a fitting setting for the long story of crimes committed against gods and men.

The story goes back a long way, for the founder of the family was Tantalus, the great King of Lydia, who, though he was admitted to the banquets of the gods, impiously attempted to test their understanding and to cheat them. He killed his son Pelops and served up the body to be eaten by his divine guests.

MYCENAE. The approach to the stronghold, seen from the Lion Gate.

At the time, Demeter was still mourning for the loss of her daughter Perse-phone. In her grief she was unobservant and ate a portion of the dead boy's shoulder. But the other gods were not mocked. Tantalus, because he had eaten of the gods' own food, was immortal; but for him this was only to mean an eternity of punishment. He was confined for ever in that part of the lower world where the greatest criminals suffer the greatest torments. As for Pelops, he was restored to life, and that portion of his shoulder which had been inadvertently devoured was replaced by a piece of ivory.

Later Pelops was driven out of Lydia by a Trojan king and came to Greece. His first exploit was the killing of King Oinomaus of Pisa. This king would insist on competing in a chariot race with all suitors for the hand of his daughter Hippodamia. The loser was to pay for his defeat with his life and, until Pelops appeared, all the suitors had lost. According to one story Pelops secured his victory by bribing Myrtilus, the king's charioteer, to loosen the linch-pins of his master's chariot, so that at the first bend of the course the chariot would fall to pieces. They say too, that when, after the victory of Pelops, Myrtilus came to claim his reward, Pelops murdered him and threw his body into the sea that bears his name.

Pelops seems to have avoided the punishment properly due for this act of treachery. He founded a great kingdom and gave the Peloponnese its name. His descendants reigned at Mycenae.

The eldest of his sons was Atreus who, by his wife, Aerope, was the father of the great princes Agamemnon and Menelaus. But Aerope was seduced by Atreus' younger brother, Thyestes, who lived secretly with her and by her became the father of other children. The guilty secret was discovered by Atreus who invited his brother to a banquet in his palace of Mycenae and then gave him to eat the cooked bodies of his own children. At the end of the meal Atreus revealed to Thyestes what it was that he had been eating. Thyestes fled from the place, overturning the table with his foot and calling down a curse on the house of Atreus. Later, again through a guilty love, he became the father of Aegisthus, who was to be instrumental in making this curse effective.

Entrance to the so-called TREASURY OF ATREUS or Tomb of Agamemnon, underground tholos tomb from the 13th century B.C. below the entrance to the citadel, with a doorway 18 ft. high.

In due course Agamemnon became King of Mycenae, and Menelaus of Sparta. The wife of Agamemnon, Clytemnestra, was the sister of Menelaus' wife Helen. Another guilty love, that of Helen and Paris, involved the brothers in the expedition against Troy.

During their ten years' absence, the foundations of the house of Atreus were undermined. First Agamemnon himself weakly listened to the advice of a soothsayer and, in order to secure good sailing weather for the fleet, sacrificed his own daughter Iphigeneia on an altar, having got the girl away from her home on the pretext of marrying her to Achilles. Clytemnestra had a grievance against her husband and she made full use of it. Thyestes' son, Aegisthus, now appeared at Mycenae and became the lover of Agamemnon's wife. When, after ten years, Agamemnon returned in triumph from Troy, he brought with him among his captives the daughter of Priam, the prophetess Cassandra. Cassandra's second sight made her shrink in horror from entering the palace. She seemed to see in front of her the mutilated bodies of children and she knew that more blood still was to flow down those walls and over that floor. As for Agamemnon, he walked into his palace on purple carpets, but in his bathroom his arms were confined in a kind of strait-jacket, and he was murdered by his wife with repeated blows of an axe. Cassandra also was killed and from then on Clytemnestra ruled over Mycenae with her lover Aegisthus openly sharing the power with her. Her daughters, the children of Agamemnon, Electra and Chrysothemis, remained with her. Her son, Orestes, had been carried into safety in the north by a faithful servant, who was to train the young boy up in thoughts of one day avenging his father's death.

When Orestes had grown to manhood Apollo himself from his oracle at Delphi instructed him, on the pain of dreadful penalties, to fulfil his task, even though it involved the killing of a mother. Orestes, to the delight of his sister, Electra, returned to Mycenae and carried out the commands of the god, killing both Clytemnestra and Aegisthus. No sooner had he done this deed, in obedience to the clear orders of Apollo, than he was himself involved in the terrible anger of different divine powers. He was haunted by the Erinyes, and driven by them in what should have been the moment of his triumph away from the palace of his fathers. Only in Athens, in a court of law presided over by Athena, could these angry goddesses be satisfied and Orestes restored to his right mind. The curse had worked itself out, but there were no more kings in Mycenae.

I have recalled briefly some aspects of this savage and subtle legend, which has so deeply affected the literature of Europe, because, when one stands on this citadel of Mycenae, it is impossible not to remember the stories with which the place is associated. Indeed, so appropriate is the place to the stories that I believe that even those who are unacquainted with them would still feel, from the landscape alone, something of their impact. Some years ago, in attempting to describe the scene, I myself wrote as follows:

'Here one may imagine Cassandra standing in terror at her second sight, the visions of slaughtered children and of further slaughter still to come. Here, perhaps, was the bath where Agamemnon was murdered; here the chamber where Clytemnestra and Aegisthus enjoyed their guilty loves; here Orestes revealed himself as an avenger and here first became aware of the pursuing presence of the Erinyes. Far more than this may be imagined on this grey rock which, in the spring, is scarlet with anemones and which, even then, has a grim aspect as though the very scarlet of the flowers was the stain of blood.

'I have seen it at all seasons and even in the sunniest weather when the air is full of the murmurs of insects, a sound interrupted continually by the distant noise of goat bells, when light drenches the two great hills between which the citadel of Mycenae stands above its steep gorges, when the grey of these mountains seems white and blazing against the blue sky and when, if one looks out to the plain of Argos below and the sea beyond, one will be survey-ing a view whose calm, flat and various extent must soothe and fascinate the eye—even then this small but immensely powerful rock seems to crouch, alert and instinct with a different kind of life, between mountains that are savage, dominating from its small stature the whole rich plain with a kind of domina-tion that is certain, uncanny and ferocious, like that exercised by a weasel over a rabbit.

'I have stood here too in grey and rainy weather when skeins of mist have hung in the gorges and blanketed the two peaks behind. In such conditions, perhaps, this ancient fastness might be expected to wear a desolate and a Gothic air. But it is not precisely so. Nothing here can be imagined of the romantic or the picturesque. Desolate, certainly, and haunted the place may seem, but with a quality that recalls nothing medieval, nothing in the novels of Sir Walter Scott.' (*Views of Attica*, pp. 116–17.)

MYCENAE

Give me your hands, give me your hands, give me your hands

I saw in the night
The mountain's pointed peak
I saw the plain afar flooded in moonlight
And no moon to be seen;
I saw, turning my head,
Black stones huddled around
And all my life stretched out like a string,
The beginning and the ending,
The final moment
My hands.

Needs must he sink who carries the great stones;
These stones I have carried as long as I was able,
These stones I have loved as long as I was able,
These stones my fate.
Wounded by my own soil
Tortured by my own garment
Condemned by my own gods,
These stones.

I know they do not know; yet I
Who have so often followed
The path that leads from murderer to victim
From victim to the punishment
And from the punishment up to another murder;
Groping my way
Over the purple welling inexhaustible
That night of the return
When the whistling began
Of Furies in the scanty grass—
I have seen snakes crossed with vipers
Knotted about the accursed generation
Our fate.

Voices out of stone, out of sleep
Voices more deep here where the world grows dark,
Memory of toil that is rooted in the rhythm
Beaten upon the earth by feet forgotten.
Bodies sunk, all naked, in the foundations
Of the other time. Eyes
Staring and staring towards a sign
That you, however you wish it, cannot distinguish.
The soul
That fights to become your soul.

Even the silence is no longer yours
Here where the mill stones have stopped still.

GEORGE SEFERIS
Translated by Rex Warner

BEYOND Aegina and a little inland from the coast of the Argolid is Epidaurus, the great centre of healing and of miraculous cures. Here was the sanctuary of Asclepius who, as we have seen, was, according to one legend, killed by a thunderbolt for bringing Hippolytus back to life. However that may be, he was soon worshipped with divine honours himself. He was a genial, even at times a humorous god; and there is plenty of evidence to show that the cures effected at Epidaurus were both genuine and numerous.

The story of the god's introduction to Athens throws a light on the difficult question of what, exactly, the Greeks thought of their deities. I cannot do better than quote the account given of it by Professor Guthrie.

'We are quite well informed about the bringing of the god to Athens, where he was introduced in 420 B.C., though a small sanctuary appears to have been in existence somewhat earlier at the harbour of Munychia. This was a time when Athens was very much in the centre of the stage of history, and many of her most famous writers were alive. We may be surprised at the amount of credulity which seems to be displayed in the introduction of this new cult in what is often regarded as the great age of Athenian enlightenment and sophistication. It may well be that enlightenment and scepticism did not go so far as we sometimes think, and it is perhaps necessary to remind our-selves that the city was not only committed to the long war that was ultimately to lead to her eclipse, but had recently lived through the horrors of a plague in addition to those of the war. These are circumstances very favourable to an exhibition of superstition or the more credulous forms of religion.

'The evidence for the event is the best possible, namely the actual contem-porary inscription commemorating it, which has been unearthed on the southern slope of the Acropolis. Mutilated though it is, it is worth many a lengthy account by some antiquarian of later centuries. It tells how the god arrived in the city from Epidaurus during the celebration of the Eleusinia. He brought his sacred serpent with him on a car, and was met by a citizen called Telemachos, who seems to have been responsible for the introduction of the cult. "Together with him came Hygieia, and thus was this whole sanctuary founded." The event is then dated in customary fashion by the name of the archon for the year.

'One of the most interesting traditions is that which assigns a prominent part in all this to the poet Sophocles. He was said to have been granted an epiphany of the god in his own house, and he composed a paean to him which continued to be sung for many years after his death. Our best authority is Plutarch, who in one passage says that Sophocles "rejoiced in the belief that he was entertaining Asklepios" and that he had an epiphany of him. In another: "There is a tradition that Sophocles even during his lifetime gave hospitality to Asklepios, a tradition in support of which there is much evidence still to be found." ' (W. K. C. Guthrie. *The Greeks and their Gods*, p. 246.)

Even today the sight of the remains of the great sanctuary at Epidaurus, and of the landscape in which the sanctuary is set, will be enough to convince one of the healing powers which this god once possessed. Now there is only a wide area of ruin among the green of pines where once stood the library, the baths, the gymnasia, the flowering columns, the porticoes with their frescoes of Love and Drunkenness. There is a stadium for athletic sports and, most perfect of the remains, there is the vast theatre, which, looked at in isolation from its surroundings, may appear, from its mere size, vulgar. But those who were sitting in it could see not only the orchestra below them, but a tremendous view extending into the distance over trees and valleys as far as the great mountains on the farther shore of the Gulf of Nauplia. It is a place which, however different from other places with a peculiar genius such as Delphi or Mycenae, has its own most calm, firm and pervasive quality.

Perhaps the games, the baths and the theatrical performances played a part in inducing an attitude of mind among the invalids which made them receptive to some form of 'faith healing'. The actual process of healing involved laying the patient down to sleep in the precinct of the god's temple. Here, during the night, he or she was, if fortunate, rewarded by a dream or vision of the god or of the snakes sacred to him. The priests, if we are to judge from the *Plutos* of Aristophanes, were often suspected of making off with the food which had been given by worshippers as an offering for the god himself. But, though the Greeks seem never to have attributed much sanctity to their priests, they still believed in their gods. Two inscriptions from Epidaurus (both quoted by Professor Guthrie) will help to make clear the nature of the belief and the genial character of the god.

(1) 'Ambrosia of Athens, blind in one eye. She came as a suppliant to the god, but as she went round the precinct she scoffed at some of the cures as incredible: it was impossible that the lame and blind should become whole simply through seeing a dream. Then she went to sleep there and saw a vision. It seemed that the god stood over her and said that he would cure her, but that he required her to set up in the temple as payment a silver pig, in memory of her stupidity. When he had said this, he cut open her blind eye and poured in ointment. And when it was day she went out cured.'

(2) 'Euphanes a boy of Epidauros. He went to sleep in the precinct suffering from stone. It seemed to him that the god stood over him and said: "What will you give if I cure you?" The boy replied: "Ten knuckle-bones." Then the god laughed and said he would cure him, and when it was day he went out whole.'

OLYMPIA AND THE OLYMPIC GAMES

THE SACRED places of Greece differ widely each from each. Nothing, for example, could be more unlike the sublime scenery of Delphi than is the plain by the river Alpheus, set in a wooded and gentle landscape, where, every four years, were held the Olympic Games.

The Games were founded in 776 B.C. and were not abolished until the reign of the Emperor Theodosius I, about twelve hundred years later. Of these games and of the other Pan-Hellenic athletic festivals, Lowes Dickinson writes as follows:

'. . . if we look more closely into the character of the public games in Greece we see that they were so surrounded and transfused by an atmosphere of imagination that their appeal must have been as much to the aesthetic as to the physical sense. For in the first place those great gymnastic contests in which all Hellas took part, and which gave the tone to their whole athletic life, were primarily religious festivals. The Olympic and Nemean Games were held in honour of Zeus, the Pythian, of Apollo, the Isthmean, of Poseidon. In the enclosures in which they took place stood temples of the gods; and sacrifice, prayer and choral hymn were the background against which they were set. And since in Greece religion implied art, in the wake of the athlete followed the sculptor and the poet. The colossal Zeus of Pheidias, the wonder of the ancient world, flashed from the precincts of Olympia its glory of ivory and gold; temples and statues broke the brilliant light into colour and form; and under that vibrating heaven of beauty, the loveliest nature crowned with the finest art, shifted and shone what was in itself a perfect type of both, the grace of harmonious motion in naked youths and men. For in Greek athletics, by virtue of the practice of contending nude, the contest itself became a work of art; and not only did sculptors draw from it an inspiration such as has been felt by no later age, but to the combatants themselves, and the spectators, the plastic beauty of the human form grew to be more than its prowess or its strength, and gymnastic became a training in aesthetics as much as, or more than, in physical excellence.

'And as with the contest, so with the reward, everything was designed to appeal to the sensuous imagination. The prize formally adjudged was symbolical only, a crown of olive; but the real triumph of the victor was the ode

127

in which his praise was sung, the procession of happy comrades, and the evening festival. . . .' (*The Greek View of Life*, p. 132.)

There were, in fact, also some more substantial rewards. In some States Olympic victors would be granted free meals for the rest of their lives and statues would be put up in their honour. And for the wealthy and ambitious the honour of having trained a winning chariot team was something very well worth having. When, for example, Alcibiades was appointed to the command in Sicily and was attacked by his political opponents for his unruly private life and for his extravagant and passionate interest in horse-racing, he defends himself, according to Thucydides, as follows:

'As for all the talk there is against me, it is about things which bring honour to my ancestors and myself, and to our country profit as well. There was a time when the Hellenes imagined that our city had been ruined by the war, but they came to consider it even greater than it really is, because of the splendid show I made as its representative at the Olympic Games, when I entered seven chariots for the chariot race (more than any private individual has entered before) and took the first, second and fourth places and saw that everything else was arranged in a style worthy of my victory. It is customary for such things to bring honour, and the fact that they are done at all must also give an impression of power.'

One of the first and legendary chariot races to take place in the plain of Elis was that between the young Pelops, founder of the house of Atreus, and King Oinomaus, who had long prevented all suitors from marrying his

---

HEAD OF HYGIEA, from Tegea in Arcadia. Perhaps from the statue in the temple of Athena Alea, which, together with the statues of Athena and Asclepius, are attributed by Pausanias to Scopas of Paros. Date, about 380 B.C. National Museum, Athens.
(*Pages 130–1*) THE THEATRE, EPIDAURUS, built by Polycletus about the middle of the 4th century. The auditorium includes three rows of seats of honour and fifty-two rows of ordinary seats, separated by a gangway and divided into wedge-shaped sections (twelve below and twenty-two above) by the mounting steps. The topmost row of seats is 194 ft. away from and 74 ft. above the orchestra. Diameter of orchestra 40 ft. The sacred precinct of Epidaurus was unearthed by Kavvadias in 1881–7.

daughter Hippodamia by insisting upon competing with them in a race. Until the time of Pelops they all lost and were all put to death by the spear of Oinomaus. Pelops was supposed in the end to have been buried at Olympia and in his first Olympian Ode, Pindar writes of him as follows:

'When he came to the sweet flower of his growth
And down covered his darkening chin,
He lifted his thoughts to a bridal awaiting him,

To have far-famed Hippodameia
From her Pisan father.
He went down beside the grey sea
In the darkness alone,
And cried to the loud-bellowing Lord of the Trident.
And the God was with him
Close beside his feet: and Pelops said:
"If the dear love you had of me, Poseidon,
Can turn, I pray, to good,
Keep fast now the brazen spear of Oinomaos,
And on the swiftest chariots carry me
To Elis, and bring me to victory;
For he has slain thirteen men that wooed her,
And put back the bridal day

Of his daughter. The danger is great,
And calls not the coward: but of us who must die,
Why should a man sit in darkness
And cherish to no end
An old age without a name,
Letting go all lovely things?
For me this ordeal waits: and you
Give me the issue I desire."

BASSAI, TEMPLE OF APOLLO, dedicated to Apollo Epicurius. Altitude 3,707 ft. Begun in the 5th century, from plans by Ictinus, completed about 400 B.C.

So he spoke, and the prayer he made was not unanswered.
The God glorified him, and gave him a chariot of gold,
And wing'd horses that never tired.
So he brought down the strength of Oinomaos,
And the maiden to share his bed.
She bore him princes,
Six sons eager in nobleness.

And now, by the ford of Alpheios,
He is drenched with the glorious blood-offerings,
With a busy tomb beside that altar
Where strangers come past number.'

(*Olympian*, I. 67–93. Tr. H. T. Wade-Gery and C. M. Bowra.)

Grandeur certainly marked the great occasions and the places 'where strangers come past number'. There was also an ordinary life which went on in this delightful landscape. Two miles from the temple of Zeus, at a place called Scillus, was once the country estate where Xenophon retired. The estate had been bought with money that had come from the sale of prisoners captured by the Ten Thousand on their march from Mesopotamia to the Black Sea. Part of the proceeds of this sale had been vowed to Apollo and to Artemis. In the end the use which Xenophon made of the money devoted to

---

OLYMPIA, PILLARS OF THE HERAEUM. This, the oldest temple at Olympia, was built at the beginning of the 7th century and dedicated to Zeus and Hera. In the 6th century Zeus received a temple of his own, and the old temple was devoted to Hera alone. The pillars were originally of wood, but were gradually replaced by stone ones. Only two of these now remain standing. The interior contained the most costly antiquities and sacred vessels of the Altis. The origin of the sanctuary in the valley of the Alpheus in the land of Elis is lost in the grey mists of prehistory. According to experts and individual research workers, it goes back to a pre-Doric age. It is an early home of the cult of Zeus. Olympiads were reckoned from the year 776 B.C.; the Olympic Games were abolished in A.D. 393. The excavation of the Altis, destroyed in part by earthquakes, was begun by the French in 1829 (metopes in the Louvre), but only in 1875–81 was it systematically carried out by the Germans under Ernst Curtius. After the removal of the debris, in some places 13 ft. high, a new grove of pines grew up.

the goddess (he had already had an offering made for Apollo and put up in the Athenian treasury at Delphi) certainly benefited him personally; but Xenophon was scrupulously correct in his dealings with the gods, as is shown by his account both of his care of this money and of his use of it. He writes:

'As for the part which belonged to Artemis of Ephesus, when Xenophon was returning from Asia on the march to Boeotia with Agesilaus, he left it in the keeping of Megabyzus, the warden of the temple of Artemis, as he thought that his journey would be a risky business. He asked Megabyzus to return the money to him if he got safe home, but if anything happened to him, he was to have something made which he thought would please the goddess, and dedicate it to her. When Xenophon had been banished and had already settled at Scillus on land near Olympia, which had been granted to him by the Spartans, Megabyzus came to Olympia to see the games and gave back the money which had been deposited with him.

'When Xenophon received it, he bought an estate as an offering to the goddess in a place where the oracle had instructed him. There happened to be a river called the Selinus which ran through the estate, and in Ephesus there is also a river Selinus, which runs past the temple of Artemis. There are fishes and shellfish in both rivers. On the estate at Scillus there is hunting also, and all kinds of game are available. Xenophon also used the sacred money for building an altar and a temple, and ever afterwards he used to take a tenth of the season's produce from the land and make a sacrifice to the goddess. All the townspeople and the men and women of the district used to take part in the festival, and the goddess provided those who camped out there with barley, bread, wine, dainties, and a share both of the animals sacrificed from the sacred herds and also of the animals caught in hunting. There were plenty of them as Xenophon's sons and the sons of other townspeople used to go

---

OLYMPIA. *Above:* The Cronion Hill and the Alpheus Valley with the Altis. *Below:* THE TEMPLE OF ZEUS, built in the second quarter of the 5th century, was 210 ft. long and had thirteen columns along the sides and six at the ends. Phidias' gold-and-ivory statue of Zeus reached a private collection in Byzantium, but perished there in a fire. The picture shows broken columns of the temple, lying as they may have been overthrown by an earthquake.

---

hunting specially for the festival, and anybody else who liked joined them in the hunt. Pig, antelopes and stag were caught, partly from the sacred land itself and partly from Mount Pholoe. The land is on the road from Sparta to Olympia, about two miles from the temple of Zeus at Olympia. In the ground sacred to Artemis there are meadows and thickly wooded hills, good breeding country for pig and goats and horses as well, and consequently it is possible to provide fodder for the animals of those who come to the festival. Round the temple itself there has been set a plantation of fruit trees which produce fruit to eat in all the appropriate seasons. The temple is a small-scale version of the great temple at Ephesus, and the image is as like the one in Ephesus as a cypress statue can be like one of gold. A pillar stands by the temple, with the following inscription on it:

'"This ground is sacred to Artemis. He who owns it and takes its produce is to offer the tenth part to Artemis every year. From the remainder he is to keep the temple in repair. Whosoever neglects to do this will not escape the notice of the goddess."'

It should be remarked that, although for much of the year one could enjoy in tranquil weather all the amenities which Xenophon describes, the Olympic Games were held in the height of summer. It was not until Roman times that an adequate supply of water was provided for the spectators. On this point there is an interesting passage in Frazer's *Pausanias and other Greek Sketches*.

'In the close hot climate of Olympia the need of a good supply of drinking water is especially felt. For months together rain hardly falls; between May

---

OLYMPIA, METOPE FROM THE TEMPLE OF ZEUS, depicting Athena. From the scene in which Heracles fetches the Stymphalian birds. The original in the Louvre, Paris.

(*Pages 140–1*) OLYMPIA, METOPES FROM THE TEMPLE OF ZEUS. *Left:* Atlas is bringing to Heracles, who is supporting the weight of the heavens on his shoulders, the Golden Apples from the Garden of the Hesperides. Olympia Museum. *Right:* Heracles, aided by Athena, is cleaning the Augean stables. Olympia Museum. Parian marble. Height of the metopes, 5 ft. 3 in. The twelve metopes represent the twelve labours of Heracles.

and October a shower is a rarity. The great festival was always held in summer (July or August), when the weather at Olympia is cloudless and the heat intense. Hence the multitudes who flocked to witness the games must have been much distressed by the dust and the burning sun, against which the spreading shade of the plane-trees in the sacred precinct could have afforded only an imperfect protection. Indeed, Lucian, doubtless with a strong touch of exaggeration, speaks of the spectators packed together and dying in swarms of thirst and of distemper contracted from the excessive drought. The water of the Alpheus is not good to drink, for even in the height of summer it holds in solution a quantity of chalky matter. The water of the Cladeus, on the other hand, is drinkable in its normal state; but even a little rain swells it and makes it run turbid for a long time. Hence it was necessary to sink wells and to bring water from a distance. This was done even in Greek times. Nine wells, some square, some round, some lined with the usual shell-limestone, others with plaques of terra-cotta, have been found at Olympia; and water was brought in aqueducts from the upper valley of the Cladeus. But in Roman times the supply was immensely improved and extended by the munificence of the wealthy sophist Herodes Atticus. Lucian tells us how the mountebank Peregrinus denounced Herodes and his aqueduct for pandering to the luxury and effeminacy of the day. It was the duty of the spectators, he said, to endure their thirst, and if need be to die of it. This doctrine proved unacceptable to his hearers, and the preacher had to run for his life pursued by a volley of stones.'

OLYMPIA. HERMES WITH THE CHILD DIONYSUS. Found on 8 May 1877 in the Heraeum at the spot where Pausanias tells us that there used to stand the statue of Hermes by the Attic sculptor Praxiteles. There was a period when this statue was believed by some scholars to be a late copy, but it is now recognized as an original.

ONE OF THE wonders of the world was the colossal statue of Zeus at Olympia in gold and ivory, the work of the Athenian sculptor Phidias. No one knows how, finally, the statue perished. It is assumed that Phidias went to Olympia in about 432 B.C., after the completion of the Parthenon and at the beginning of the war between Athens and Sparta, when he and other friends of Pericles were in exile on various charges. Not a single work of Phidias survives, nor, it seems, can we ever know what was the effect of the gold and the ivory which so delighted the ancient world. It is possible that the body of the statue might have survived, had Caligula been able to carry out his plan of transporting it to Rome and having his own head substituted for that of Zeus. But the ship designed to carry off the great statue was struck by Zeus' own lightning. However, some idea at least of the purpose of the sculptor and of the effect of his work on other minds can be obtained from the testimony of those who were happy enough to have seen the figure that was the great pride of the holy place. And, in considering the remains of Olympia today, it will not be out of place to recall the past. Frazer writes as follows:

'The testimony of antiquity to the extraordinary beauty and majesty of the image is very strong. The Roman general Paulus Aemilius was deeply moved by the sight of it; he felt as if in the presence of the god himself, and declared that Phidias alone had succeeded in embodying the Homeric conception of Zeus. Cicero says that Phidias fashioned the image, not after any living model, but after that ideal beauty which he saw with the inward eye alone. Quintilian asserts that the beauty of the image served to strengthen religion, the majesty of the image equalling the majesty of the god. A poet declared that either the god must have come from heaven to earth to show Phidias his image, or that Phidias must have gone to heaven to behold it. The statue was reckoned one of the seven wonders of the world, and to die without having seen it was deemed a misfortune. The rhetorician Dio Chrysostom, a man of fine taste,

OLYMPIA. *Above:* Hall of Pillars of the PALAESTRA; 3rd century. *Below:* THE ARCHED APPROACH TO THE STADIUM mentioned by Pausanias.

extolled it in one of his speeches. He calls it "the most beautiful image on earth and the dearest to the gods". He represents Phidias speaking of his "peaceful and gentle Zeus, the overseer, as it were, of united and harmonious Greece, whom by the help of my art and of the wise and good city of Elis I set up, mild and august in an unconstrained attitude, the giver of life and breath and all good things, the common father and saviour of mankind". And again in a fine passage he says: "Methinks that if one who is heavy laden in mind, who has drained the cup of misfortune and sorrow in life, and whom sweet sleep visits no more, were to stand before this image, he would forget all the griefs and troubles that are incident to the life of man." ' (*Pausanias and other Greek Sketches.*)

OLYMPIA, THE NIKE OF PAEONIUS. Found in 1875 and pieced together from many fragments. Parian marble. Height to top of head 7 ft. The Descending Nike is from a victory monument set up by the Messenians and Naupactians in honour of Zeus. It stood on a 30-ft. high plinth opposite the temple of Zeus. Ionic, by Paeonius of Mende (Thrace). Date, second half of 5th century, Olympia Museum.

CHAERONEA

ONE OF THE routes from Athens to Delphi goes round the north of Parnassus to Amphissa and, after passing through the great olive forests between Amphissa and the sea, ascends steeply to the holy place. If one takes this route one will pass, at the extremity of the Boeotian plain, the battlefield of Chaeronea and the great stone lion set up in the plain to commemorate the victory of Philip of Macedon over the Athenians and Thebans in 338 B.C.

It is a place which recalls the past and the future, since this victory marked the end of one age and the beginning of another. The period of the independent city states, with their brilliant achievements, was over; the period of an expanding Hellenism, which was to spread throughout the world, was about to begin. Philip had done what Athens might conceivably have done, if she had won the Peloponnesian War. He had organized a State which was economically and militarily irresistible, and was able to take upon himself the 'leadership' of Hellas which had for so long been disputed between Athens, Sparta, and Thebes. Macedon was a land power, like Sparta, but the enterprise and the ambitions of the Macedonians were like those of Athens. When Philip himself, two years after the battle of Chaeronea, was murdered, he was already planning to lead a great Hellenic force to the east. But his policy was not interrupted by his death. In 334 his son Alexander, at the age of twenty-two, crossed the Hellespont with an army of 40,000 men. Though Demosthenes was unaware of the fact, the old days had gone, never to return. Far beyond the farthest journeys of Xenophon and the Ten Thousand, new Hellenic cities were to spring up throughout the east. The young conqueror left his name not only in the great and splendid city of Alexandria in Egypt.

OLYMPIA, FROM THE WEST PEDIMENT OF THE TEMPLE OF ZEUS. A scene from the wedding of the King of the Lapithae disturbed by the Centaurs: Hippodamia, the bride of Pirithous, is being carried off by the Centaur Eurytus. (According to a later description: double wedding in the house of King Dexamenus of Elis between his daughters, Theronike and Theraiphone, and the Actoridae Eurytus and Cteatus. Apollo orders the Actoridae to avenge the crime of the Centaurs who had attacked the brides and the maidens during the wedding feast.) Head of a Lapith fighting with a Centaur.

There were other Alexandrias by the Cilician Gates, in Afghanistan, in Khorasan and by the Jaxartes. And along with this tremendous political and cultural expansion came signs of a totally new outlook. Alexander began to believe that he was a god and in 324 B.C. instructed the Greek cities to treat him as such. It may well have been that Alexander, who was, after all, a pupil of Aristotle, had doubts about how these claims would be accepted, but it seems likely that he believed in them himself.

Not only Demosthenes, but many others must have been bewildered by the new world which was dawning and must have resented the sweeping away of so much that had been regarded as essentially and eternally Hellenic. Certainly the Spartans seem to have been content to hug the memories of their greatness and were as reluctant as ever to welcome any departure from the old ways. After the great victory of the Granicus, Alexander went out of his way to show his feelings for this conservative race which had sent no contingents to his army. Plutarch, who, many years later, was born at and lived in Chaeronea, describes the magnitude of the victory and the gesture of Alexander as follows:

'The Persians lost in this battle twenty thousand foot and two thousand five hundred horse. On Alexander's side, Aristobulus says, there were not wanting above four-&-thirty, of whom nine were foot soldiers; and in memory of them he caused so many statues of brass, of Lysippus' making, to be erected. And that the Grecians might participate in the honour of his victory he sent a portion of the spoils home to them, particularly to the Athenians three hundred bucklers, and upon all the rest he ordered this inscription to be set: "Alexander, the son of Philip, and the Grecians, except the Lacedae-monians, won these from the barbarians who inhabit Asia."' (*Life of Alexander*, Tr. Dryden.)

A modern Greek poet, C. P. Cavafy, himself a native of Alexandria in Egypt, has written a fine poem on this theme. The poem is called 'In the year

OLYMPIA, FROM THE WEST PEDIMENT OF THE TEMPLE OF ZEUS.
Hippodamia, the bride of Pirithous, being carried off by a Centaur. Marble. Larger than life-size. Olympia Museum (cf. page 155).

200 B.C.', and in it the poet imagines a Greek of that time (a hundred and thirty years after the great victories), reading the inscription and contrasting the narrowness of the Spartans with the tremendous achievement of the Helleniza⁄tion of Asia. The poem is as follows:

'We are able very well to imagine
How completely unaffected they must have been at Sparta
By that inscription: "Excepting the Lacedaemonians!"
But naturally. They were not, the Spartans,
To be led about, and to be ordered about
Like valuable servants. And besides
A panhellenic expedition without
A Spartan king for leader
Would not have appeared to them of much standing.
O most certainly "excepting the Lacedaemonians".

That too is an attitude. It can be understood.

And so, "excepting the Lacedaemonians" at the Granikos;
And afterwards at Issos; and at the final
Battle, where was swept away the fearful host
Which the Persians had concentrated at Arbela,
Which moved off from Arbela for victory, and was swept away.

And out of that wonderful panhellenic expedition,
The victorious, the illustrious,
The renowned, the glorified
As none has been glorified else,
The incomparable expedition: we have come out
A new Greek world and great.

We: the Alexandrians, the men of Antioch,
The Seleucians, and the numerous
Greeks over above of Aegypt and of Syria,
And those of Media, and those in Persia, and all the others.

152

With our far-reaching dominations,
With various influence prudently adapted,
And our Greek Common Speech.
Into the midst of Bactria we carried it, even to the Indians.

Talk about the Lacedaemonians now!'

                              (C. P. Cavafy. Tr. J. Mavrogordato.)

DELPHI

THE FOLLOWING description, taken from Frazer, of the scenery of Delphi has the great merits of clarity and accuracy. But it must be remembered that no description can give more than a faint idea of the grandeur and sublimity of this tremendous scene.

'The site of Delphi, till lately occupied by the modern village of Kastri, is in the highest degree striking and impressive. The city lay at the southern foot of the tremendous cliffs of Parnassus, which form a sheer wall of rock, about eight hundred feet high. Over these frightful precipices Philomelus drove some of the defeated Locrians. Just at the angle where this vast wall of rock bends round towards the south it is met from top to bottom by a deep and gloomy gorge, some twenty feet wide, where there is a fine echo. Facing each other across this narrow chasm rise two stupendous cliffs, whose peaked summits tower considerably above the rest of the line of cliffs. They are nearly perpendicular in front, and perfectly so where they fall sheer down into the gorge. The eastern of the two cliffs was called Hyampia in antiquity; from its top Aesop is said to have been hurled by the Delphians. It has been suggested, though perhaps without sufficient reason, that when the later writers of antiquity, especially the Roman poets, speak of the two summits of Parnassus, they are really referring to these two cliffs. In point of fact the cliffs are far indeed from being near the summit of Parnassus; but seen from Delphi they completely hide the higher slopes of the mountain. In winter or wet weather a torrent comes foaming down the gorge in a cascade about two hundred feet high, bringing down the water from the higher slopes of the mountain. At the mouth of the gorge, under the eastern cliff, is the rock-cut basin of the perennial Castalian spring, a few paces above the highway. The water from the spring joins the stream from the gorge, which, after passing over the road, plunges into a deep rocky lyn or glen, which it has scooped out for itself in the steep side of the mountain. Down this glen the stream descends to join the

---

OLYMPIA, FROM THE WEST PEDIMENT OF THE TEMPLE OF ZEUS. Central figure, 10 ft. 2 in. in height. Marble. Olympia Museum (cf. page 150).

Plistus, which flows along the bottom of the Delphic valley from east to west, at a great depth below the town.

'From the cliffs at the back of Delphi the ground slopes away so steeply to the bed of the Plistus that it is only by means of a succession of artificial terraces rising in tiers above each other, that the soil can be cultivated and made fit for habitation. There are about thirty of these terraces, supported by stone walls, mostly of polygonal masonry. The sanctuary of Apollo occupies only the five or six highest terraces at the foot of the cliffs, on the western side of the Castalian gorge. So high does it stand above the bottom of the valley that twenty minutes are needed to descend the steep terraced slope to the bed of the Plistus. Corn is grown on the terraces below the sanctuary; and the slopes on the eastern side of the Castalian gorge are wooded with fine olive and mulberry trees. Across the valley, on the southern side of the Plistus, rise the bare precipitous cliffs of Mount Cirphis, capped with fir-woods. From the western end of the precipices which rise at the back of Delphi a high rocky ridge projects southward towards the bed of the Plistus. This ridge closes the valley of Delphi on the west, shutting out all the view of the Crisaean plain and the Gulf of Corinth, though a glimpse of the waters of the gulf is obtained from the stadium, the highest part of Delphi.

'Thus, enclosed by a rocky ridge on the west, by tremendous precipices on the north and east, and faced on the south, across the valley of the Plistus, by the lower but still precipitous sides of Mount Cirphis, Delphi lay in a secluded mountain valley; and rising on terraces in a semi-circular shape, it resembled an immense theatre, to which it has justly been compared by ancient and modern writers. The whole scene is one of stern and awful majesty, well fitted to be the seat of a great religious capital. In respect of natural scenery no contrast could well be more striking than that between the two great religious capitals of ancient Greece, Delphi and Olympia—Delphi clinging to the rugged side of barren mountains, with frowning precipices above and a pro-found glen below; Olympia stretched out on the level margin of a river that winds in stately curves among the cornfields and vineyards of a smiling valley set between soft wooded hills.' (J. G. Frazer. *Pausanias and other Greek Sketches.*)

OLYMPIA, FROM THE EAST PEDIMENT OF THE TEMPLE OF ZEUS.
Head of an old man (a seer) from the right half. Olympia Museum.

There are some other elements in the scene at Delphi which have not been mentioned by Frazer in this passage. There are, for example, the eagles which are constantly to be seen wheeling in the high air above the eight hundred feet of rock behind the sanctuary, gliding over the face of the rock, or flying below the level of the eye above the olives in the deep valley of the Plistus. The birds are common in these mountains and are a part of the scene, whether soaring in the sunlight or, as sometimes happens, emerging suddenly out of the mist in front of one's car on gigantic wings, and seeming to threaten, before gliding back again into the clouds, both the vehicle and its occupants. Then, too, Frazer's reference to 'fine olive trees' scarcely does justice to the tremendous river of green and silver that flows down the valley of the Plistus to join that other wider stream of olives from Amphissa. It is possible too that a reader of Frazer's excellent description may not realize from it how high above the valley Delphi clings to the mountains; for Frazer, it seems to me, must have been gifted with quite exceptional agility if he was able to make the descent from the sanctuary to the Plistus in the short time of twenty minutes.

THE ORACLE

THERE WERE divine powers older than Apollo and the Olympians. Orestes, as we have seen, though clearly instructed by Apollo to take his mother's life in retribution for her crime against her husband, could not escape the avenging deities whose function it was to punish, above all things, the shedding of a mother's blood. These older deities were female and reflected, in many of their aspects, the earlier matriarchal system of society of the Mediterranean world. Even at Delphi, it seems, Apollo did not establish himself without a struggle, and, in contrast to the usual practice among the Olympians by which a god was served by a priest and a goddess by a priestess, at Delphi the god spoke through the mouth of a woman. In the Homeric Hymn to Pythian Apollo, the young god has to fight with a great serpent, an evil monster who has been in league with Hera against Zeus, before he can establish himself at Delphi. Aeschylus, at the beginning of the *Eumenides*, makes the Pythia (Apollo's prophetess) state clearly that the first prophetess was Earth, who was succeeded in the prophetic seat by her daughter Themis; then came another child of Earth, the Titaness Phoebe, who voluntarily handed over her position as a birthday gift to Apollo, who took from her the name 'Phoebus'. Aeschylus is always, and particularly in this play, concerned to 'justify the ways of god' and it is natural for him to overlook any ugly story of violence in heaven. With him even the story of Prometheus seems to have ended in a reconciliation. Euripides, on the other hand, retains the version of the story which includes Apollo's battle with the serpent.

Archaeology supports the evidence of tradition. To quote Professor Parke:

'Excavation has shown that the site was occupied freely in Late Minoan times, and an object used in Minoan ritual—a limestone vessel for pouring, shaped like a lioness's head—was actually found in the site of the classical sanctuary. Evidently this place, otherwise unattractive for habitation, was frequented as early as 1500 B.C. and had become a centre of cult. The subject of Minoan religion cannot be fully elucidated through the surviving monuments and the traces in classical tradition, but all indications point to the conclusion that the chief deity of the Minoans and those influenced by them on the Greek mainland was at all times a goddess, strongly associated with the earth and its fruits. Hence, if Delphi was a cult centre before Hellenic times, an original worship of an earth goddess there would be a natural supposition on our archaeological evidence alone.' (H. W. Parke. *A History of the Delphic Oracle*.)

It is probable too that the famous Omphalos, an egg-shaped stone which was kept in the most holy place of the temple, had something to do with the worship of Earth. By the Greeks of later times this Omphalos was regarded as marking the navel or centre of the earth, and the geographical discovery was attributed to Zeus who set free two eagles, one from each extremity of earth and observed that the birds, flying on a straight course and at a uniform speed, met over Delphi.

It has been suggested also that the ecstasy of the Pythia, her apparent 'possession' by the god, is evidence of the earlier Minoan religion. This may be so, though the worshippers of Dionysus also were 'possessed' by their god, and Dionysus was a later arrival on the scene even than Apollo. It is certainly strange, or it would be strange if the whole aspect of Greece were not full of such contradictions, to find Apollo, who is pre-eminently the god of sanity, of order and of clarity, speaking in his chief sanctuary through the mouth of a female who, unless viewed, as she was viewed, with the eyes of religious reverence, must have appeared completely out of her right mind.

How exactly the Pythia became 'possessed' we do not know. None of the various rationalistic 'explanations' which have been given in ancient or modern times explain everything. One theory supposes that vapour with intoxicating properties emerged from a chasm on which the prophetess hung suspended. But, in the first place, there is no chasm; and as for the vapour, Professor Parke declares:

'Geologically it is quite impossible at Delphi where the limestone and schist could not have emitted a gas with any intoxicating properties.'

CHAERONEA. The Lion which commemorates the defeat of the Athenians and Thebans by Philip of Macedon in 338 B.C. Re-erected from broken sections, 1902–3. Height of figure nearly 20 ft.

(Pages 162–3) DELPHI. View from the level of the theatre over the sanctuary, built on a succession of terraces, and across the valley of the Plistus with its olive groves.

Nor could the Pythia have reached a state of ecstasy by the chewing of laurel leaves. To quote Professor Parke again:

'The leaves of some shrubs which could be named "laurel" are bitter to the taste, and actually contain a little prussic acid, but the proportion is too minute to have any toxic effect on an individual.'

What we know for certain is that the Pythia, when she was delivering the responses, was believed to be and believed herself to be, a vehicle for the divine power of Apollo. Probably the best imaginative account of such a state is to be found in Virgil's description of the 'possession' by the god of the prophetess at Cumae. There would have been many symptoms of what we should call 'hysteria', and at Delphi there were various ritual practices which were no doubt designed to put the Pythia into a state suitable for 'possession'. For instance one of the preliminary ceremonies was the sacrifice of a goat; but the goat was not pronounced fit to be sacrificed until it began to tremble in every limb, thus indicating, one imagines, that the god was near at hand and would soon also produce these symptoms of trembling in the Pythia herself. If the goat obdurately refused to tremble, the priests sprinkled it with cold water. The god then took possession of his human vehicle and the responses given by the Pythia were given in a state of trance or of frenzy. This phenomenon of 'possession' is certainly difficult to explain by means of the assumptions of modern materialistic science. It will also seem strange to those who have been educated to believe that the ancient Greeks were a people with one-track rationalistic minds. However, we must accept the fact that it was a phenomenon which actually took place, and we should remember that similar phenomena still take place in some parts of the world today. Among those who take part in the Voodoo rites of Haiti, for example, 'possession' is a common enough occurrence.

Since it was an ordinary enough thing to consult the oracle at Delphi, it is not surprising that we have so few accounts of the actual behaviour of the Pythia. It was something accepted and well known. There is, however, one very interesting account of an occasion when things did not go as might have

---

DELPHI. *Above:* The Theatre. Beyond, the Temple of Apollo and view of the valley of the Plistus. *Below:* Olive grove.

---

been expected. It is an account which shows clearly enough the genuineness of some form of 'possession' and it is very well authenticated. The story is told by Plutarch, and Nicander, who was priest at Delphi on the occasion, was Plutarch's personal friend. I cannot do better than quote Professor Parke's version of the story with his comments upon it.

'Some ambassadors had arrived from abroad to consult the oracle, but the goat which was to be used to test whether the oracle was auspicious remained motionless and unresponsive through the first libations poured on it. However, the priests wished to please their enquirers: important visitors were all too rare. They persisted till the victim, drenched with cold water, at last succumbed and gave the sign. The Pythia descended into the oracular chamber unwilling and dispirited. As soon as she gave her first replies the harshness of her voice revealed that she was "full of a dumb and evil spirit". At last her confusion reached its height, and with an incomprehensible and terrifying shout she threw herself toward the doorway. The ambassadors, the prophet Nicander, and the other priests in attendance, fled. After a few minutes they re-entered the room and found the Pythia restored to her normal consciousness. She was picked up, but only survived for a few days.

'Plutarch records this tragic episode so as to illustrate how serious it might be to disregard the proper preliminaries which showed whether the Pythia was fit for her function or not. For us, however, the importance is that it gives a fairly trustworthy account of a Pythia in the act of prophesying. Unfortunately, this particular incident was exceptional, and so may not be safe to use for broad generalizations. Yet there is no doubt that in this incident the Pythia was a victim, not an impostor. Also the episode offers some interesting analogies with features of modern consultations of spiritualistic mediums.' (*A History of the Delphic Oracle*, pp. 35–36.)

Of course the responses given by the Pythia in her state of trance were often more or less incoherent. They had to be 'edited' and were often put into hexameters by the priests. At this point obviously there was room for human and deliberate interference in transmitting the messages of the god. Indeed,

DELPHI. View from the sanctuary over the valley of the Plistus.

even if there were no deliberate trickery, it would be natural for the priests to prefer that the god should say one thing rather than another and to read into the Pythia's words what they wanted to see there. And there does, in fact, seem to have been a fairly consistent Delphic foreign policy, which may well have been based on accurate information and the skilful assessing of it. It is true that Delphi seems to have miscalculated with regard to the Persian invasion, but either the god or the priests chose the winning side in the Peloponnesian War and in the case of Philip of Macedon. Yet the replies of the oracle were by no means confined to matters of high policy, of colonization or of the proper ordering of religious cults. The Pythia could also be consulted by private individuals with regard to their own affairs. The best known of these replies, and the one most difficult to explain, is that which was given to Chaerephon who asked the Pythia whether there was anyone wiser than Socrates and who was informed that no one was wiser. It is extremely probable (though not certain) that this reply was given at a time when Socrates was not more than thirty-five years old. It is unlikely that at this time he could have been well known at Delphi and, if he was known, his reputation would not have been of the kind that would have commended him to a conservative religious organization. Yet the reply was undoubtedly given and, though Socrates was puzzled when he heard of it, he took it so seriously that it affected the whole course of his life. Thus this particular and mysterious reply was, as Professor Parke says, 'probably more important as a contribution to human thought than any other words that emanated from the Pythia'.

Indeed there is very much that is mysterious in the history of the oracle, much that will make the enquirer revise any easy or summary views which he may have held about the character of the ancient Greeks and of their religion. One strange element, for example, in the cult at Delphi is the important position of Dionysus in the temple of Apollo. The grave of Dionysus was shown in Apollo's sanctuary and for the three winter months it was assumed that Apollo was away and that Dionysus had taken his place in Delphi.

DELPHI. STATUE OF A CHARIOTEER. According to the inscription it is the offering of Polyzalus, tyrant of Gela, for a chariot victory in Delphi in 474 B.C. The eyes are of paste with brown irises. The lips were originally overlaid with small silver plates. Height 5 ft. 11 in. Delphi Museum.

During these winter months were held the trieteric festivals or 'orgies' in honour of Dionysus in which women from Delphi and from other Greek states worshipped, in their ecstatic way, the god upon the mountains. Though our information about these 'orgies' is far from adequate, we know enough to be sure that few, if any, of the civilized women of our day would have been physically capable of taking part in them. The band of worshippers, or Thyiads, for instance, who came from Athens had in front of them a walk of some hundred miles, with freezing weather at night and often by day, over mountain passes which might be blocked with snow. Delphi itself is high enough in the mountains, but the festivals by night were held high above Delphi after an exceptionally steep climb to the Corycian cave. Such 'orgies' as there may have been must often have taken place in deep snow. Yet, as we know from Euripides' *Bacchae* and from other sources, the orgies were both real and religious.

Dionysus was the latest of the Olympians, and, as many stories show, the new god met with considerable resistance. But it was always the policy of Delphi to spread this ecstatic worship, which, in many ways, seems so unlikely a thing to be so closely associated with Apollo. A great many oracles survive which commend the new religion. I cannot resist quoting an account (again from Professor Parke) of one of these. Like the reply given to Chaerephon, it illustrates not only the attitude of Delphi but also the attitude of those who sought advice there.

'A good historic example where Delphi chose to put forward the honour of Dionysus in preference to others is presented by the cult of Dionysus Phallenos on Lesbos. Some fishermen at Methymna brought up in their nets a face made out of olive wood. Its appearance suggested something divine, but bore no relation to any of the recognized gods of Greece. The men of Methymna consulted the Pythia to what god or hero the likeness belonged: the answer was an instruction to worship it as Dionysus Phallenos:

DELPHI. THOLOS, a circular building in the sanctuary of Athena Pronaia. Marble. Beginning of the 4th century.

(Pages 172–3) BATTLE BETWEEN THE ATHENIANS AND THE AMAZONS, from the frieze of the Athenian treasure house. End of the 4th century. Delphi Museum.

' "But it would be much better for the dwellers in Methymna, if they honour the head of Dionysus Phallenos."

'This they did, keeping the wooden original themselves and setting up a bronze copy at Delphi as a memorial.' (*A History of the Delphic Oracle*, p. 338.)

So many and so interesting are the various replies of the oracle, sometimes obscure, sometimes diplomatic, sometimes full of a delightful common sense, that one is tempted to devote more space to them than is appropriate to these short notes. But however far one might pursue the subject, an element of mystery would remain. It would seem that the flame of prophecy flickered and gradually died out rather with the decay of religious faith than for any political reasons. After the eclipse of the city states and of the empire of Alexander and his successors the oracle still continued to function. It advised the young Cicero, for instance, to think less of his audience and more of himself. It advised Nero, who, incidentally, robbed Delphi of five hundred bronze statues, to 'beware of the seventy-third' year, and the young emperor was delighted. He did not think of the old man Galba, who, at the age of seventy-two, launched a successful revolt and took the empire from him. Later still, in attempting to satisfy the literary curiosity of the Emperor Hadrian, the oracle gave the surprising information that Homer was the grandson of Odysseus and was born in Ithaca. But long before the time of Hadrian it is evident that the importance of the oracle had declined, and its temporary revival was artificial. By the time that Christianity became the official religion the Pythia had become silent. Perhaps, for a period, the priests remained; but when Julian the Apostate attempted to revive the rites of Delphi, he only received from them a discouraging answer to the effect that Phoebus had gone for ever, and no more prophecies could be expected in the future.

OLYMPUS, mountain peak (9,574 ft. high) in Thessaly, the legendary seat of the Olympian gods. (Photo: Boissonnas.)

ACKNOWLEDGMENTS

Thanks are due to the publishers concerned for permission to quote from the under-mentioned works:

Rex Warner, *Views of Attica* (John Lehmann); Rex Warner, *The Medea* and *The Hippolytus* of Euripides (John Lane, The Bodley Head); Rex Warner, *The Pelopon-nesian War* of Thucydides and *The Anabasis of Xenophon* (Penguin Classics); Osbert Lancaster, *Classical Landscape with Figures* (John Murray); W. K. C. Guthrie, *The Greeks and their Gods* (Methuen); H. W. Parke, *A History of the Delphic Oracle* (Black-well); *The Poems of Cavafy*, tr. J. Mavrogordato (Hogarth Press); *The Oxford Book of Greek Verse in Translation*, ed. T. F. Higham and C. M. Bowra (Oxford University Press); George Seferis, *Mycenae* (John Lane, The Bodley Head).